JONATHAN W. MANGBON

# MY WORK AT STAKE

(STRIKING LESSON SERIES TWO)

Trafford
PUBLISHING®

Order this book online at www.trafford.com
or email orders@trafford.com

Most Trafford titles are also available at major online book retailers.

Edited by Mrs. Selina M. Mangbon &
Mrs. Awaogu C. O. Head of Department of Languages.

Note for Librarians: A cataloguing record for this book is available from Library and Archives Canada at www.collectionscanada.ca/amicus/index-e.html

Printed in Victoria, BC, Canada.

ISBN: 978-1-4251-6634-2

*Our mission is to efficiently provide the world's finest, most comprehensive book publishing service, enabling every author to experience success. To find out how to publish your book, your way, and have it available worldwide, visit us online at www.trafford.com/10510*

*Trafford rev: 2/1/2010*

www.trafford.com
**North America & International**
toll-free: 1 888 232 4444 (USA & Canada)
phone: 250 383 6864 ♦ fax: 812 355 4082

# PREFACE

THIS BOOK IS ONE OF THE SEVERAL MANUSCRIPTS written by the same author under a common caption known as 'Striking Lessons Series'. They are all works of fiction, with very striking lessons focusing on the high rate of moral decadence in the society. They contain challenging ideas to be reflected upon by the readers for possible retreats. This is aimed at grooming the society for better living. The books are all written in simple English and are good materials for elementary literatures.

"My work at stake" being the second in the series was written to portray the detrimental effects of carelessness, silly mistakes, illiteracy, gossips, cruelty, stealing, unfaithfulness at work, greediness, and uncontrolled lust. On the other hand, it promulgates the showering of blessings for faithfulness and dedications.

Other manuscripts in the series include:-
(i)   Drink and the Innocent Policeman.
(ii)  Total Confusion (a play).
(iii) Search for perfect peace.
(iv)  Test for true love.
(v)   Leave vengeance to God.
(vi)  Driven into reality.

This book is a work of fiction. The characters are imaginary, any resemblance to actual persons is accidental.

For further information or permissions, please contact the author Mr. Jonathan W. Mangbon of:

i. Kauna Baptist Church, P.O Box 572, Jalingo, Taraba State, Nigeria.

ii. Empowerment Centre for the Needy,No.123 Hammaruwa way, Mayo-gwoi, P.O 572 Jalingo, Taraba State, Nigeria.

iii. E-mail, survivalaid@hotmail.com, empowermentcentre2002@yahoo.com

iv. Telephone 08025337484,08024023456, 07030232644

# DEDICATION

*To our heavenly father, the giver of all talents to mankind.*

# TABLE OF CONTENTS

PREFACE                                             III

DEDICATION                                          V

CHAPTER ONE. DANGEROUS MISTAKE                      1

CHAPTER TWO. THE REPERCUSSIONS                      6

CHAPTER THREE. THE HANDING OVER
                    PROCESS                         15

CHAPTER FOUR. DANGEROUS GOSSIP                      22

CHAPTER FIVE. AT DOCTOR MALI'S
CONSULTING ROOM                                     28

CHAPTER SIX. HOW KINGSBAY AND ADINI'S
                    HUSBAND BECAME FRIENDS          32

CHAPTER SEVEN. MR. CUNNY'S
                    NONE PHYSICAL DISEASE           37

CHAPTER EIGHT. THE PAYMENT DEAL                     43

CHAPTER NINE. THE DRUG DELIVERY
                    DEAL                            50

CHAPTER TEN. THE JUDGMENT                           58

CHAPTER ELEVEN. CHRISTOPHER'S WIFE
                    NEEDS MEDICAL ATTENTION         62

CHAPTER TWELVE. THE DOCTOR

      ENGAGED?            66

CHAPTER THIRTEEN. CHRISTOPHER'S

      FIRST SON           70

CHAPTER FOURTEEN. AT THE

      COMPOUND OFFICE    75

CHAPTER FIFTEEN. THE LOCKED DRAWER 82

CHAPTER SIXTEEN. THE WANTED MURVI  86

CHAPTER SEVENTEEN. MURVI OUTSIDE

      THE GATE            92

CHAPTER EIGHTEEN. A DANGEROUS BAIL 99

CHAPTER NINETEEN. SEGUN'S SINCERE

      CONFESSION         105

CHAPTER TWENTY. SULE PICKED

      HIS LUCK            112

CHAPTER TWENTY-ONE. SULE'S

      DUST BIN            123

CHAPTER TWENTY-TWO. THE MYSTERIOUS

      MONEY            128

CHAPTER TWENTY-THREE. SULE AND

      AMINA            135

CHAPTER TWENTY-FOUR. THE RESCUE

      EXERCISE           140

# CHAPTER ONE

## DANGEROUS MISTAKE

DOCTOR MALI AN NYSC MEMBER was serving in Timbo Hospital. He was on call one night, attending to two very serious cases in the female medical ward. The two women, namely Sima and Martina were on danger list, both needed blood before operation. The case of old mother Sima was worse, and that is why the doctor was more concerned about her, compared to the attention being given to Martina.

Both women had streams of relatives trooping into the Hospital to see them. Most of them came to offer their blood to their respective patients if possible. Unfortunately for old mother Sima, none of her relatives had a marching blood group to hers. Her son Abu who was always by her side, became discouraged. He didn't know who else to approach for blood donation to his beloved mother. He hated the idea of becoming a complete orphan, if his mother eventually died. He was badly worried and restless.

In Martina's, case, luck was on her side. She had a sister by name Sofa who was taking care of her. Sofa's husband came to visit them and fortunately his blood group was found to march Martina's.

That evening, Dr. Mali saw the blood bag full of blood lying on a table. It was meant for old mother Sima. He was happy that the old mother was lucky at last. "Oh! so she got the blood at last" The doctor uttered in his mind. "She could then be operated upon tomorrow". He straightaway booked Sima for operation the next day. The Doctor really pitied mother

Sima because her case was a long pending one. She needed more blood in her body to enable her withstand the operation. Her condition was very critical, and unless she got the blood soonest, she might die. She had grown very lean.

At the initial stage of her sickness, many women attributed it to the effect of her husband's death. Sima had loved her husband very much. When he died, she subjected herself to much crying. All sort of persuasions from neighbouring women to stop her from crying fell on deaf ears. She cried until she lost her voice. Her eyes became swollen and blood red. Consequently, as the neigbouring women saw it, soon after the husband's death Sima began to lose weight greatly.

The usually huge and plump woman, soon started showing countable ribs and conspicuously bulging clavicle bones. Her usual beautiful round face, soon gave way to an ugly, deeply sunken and bony one. In her sick bed, Sima looked more or less like a greatly malnourished sick baboon. Her eyes had turned snow white. Apart from being seriously anaemic, she was also greatly dehydrated.

With the required blood now available, the doctor had hope that old mother Sima might live after all, but unfortunately, there was a mistake.

"My husband's blood has been tested and it marches your blood group sister" Sofa happily announced to Martina; "You will soon have the blood for your operation"."Oh! thank God" Martina Whispered in a low sick voice.

In Sima's case, Abu had gone out in search of blood donors for her. A female ward attendant came around. She picked up Sima's bedhead ticket and proceeded to Martina's bed. She beckoned Sofa's husband to follow her to the laboratory. It was for the blood donation. He followed her straight away. Sofa also accompanied them.

"Where is the blood bag you were to buy? "the lab technician asked Sofa.

"Here it is" Sofa said and happily handed one new blood bag to the lab technician.

"Good, you can now leave us alone to finish the rest" the technician pleaded. Sofa obeyed and quietly moved out of the laboratory. The ward attendant gave him the bed head ticket she brought from the ward and she walked out. Sofa and her husband didn't know the use of the bed-head ticket that was brought to the lab technician. Picking up the bed head ticket, the lab technician neatly copied out all the particulars on it unto the blood bag for identification. Such particulars included name, bed number, etc.

The unfortunate thing was that the ward attendant had brought into the lab, Sima's bedhead ticket instead of Martina's. The ward attendant was semi- literate. She could hear and speak a bit of English. She couldn't read or write. She attended primary school but got to class four only. The reason for not completing her primary education was best known to her immediate employer. The man felt that was the best way of compensating her parents for the damage caused to their daughter. The best she knew in the ward was taking orders from the Nurses; washing dirty ward dresses; beddings (used by the patients) cleaning windows and the floor. When idle, she usually spent time thinking of her only son who was killed by firing squad. That was the child she got for the man who employed her as ward attendant. The boy was the first and the last child she ever had. He dubiously grew up and became an armed robber and ended up facing the gun at last.

At last the ward attendant later came out and collected both the bag full of blood and the bed-head ticket. She took them back to the ward and placed them on a small table. It was on this table that Dr. Mali saw the blood.

Sofa had gone out to escort her husband who had to leave immediately after donating the blood. She soon came back. Abu was still in town searching for those who could donate blood to his mother Sima.

The nursing sister in-charge of the ward was busy counting the government revenue realized for that day. There was an observation in Timbo Hospital that nearly all the revenue collectors were dubious. The nursing sisters incharge were therefore directed to crosscheck all the receipts and ensure that money paid were accurately accounted for during their shifts. They were to count and keep proper records to reduce cases of revenue diversion. The Nursing sister was too busy to notice what was going on in her ward at that moment.

One of the nurses picked up the bag of blood and proceeded to Sima's bed. He was guided by the written particulars on the blood bag which corresponded to those on the bed-head ticket. Though it took the nurse much time to trace Sima's veins, he succeeded at long last to start the blood dripping in.

Abu was disappointed. He couldn't find a good Samaritan that would donate blood to his mother. He was ready to pay any amount for a marching blood to save his mother's life. He was Sima's first born. His father died when he was over twenty-one years old. Right from youth, Abu loved to do business. He went deep into business quite early enough, becoming well established by the time his mother was hospitalized. Money was not his problem. He only wanted his mother to be well at all cost to avoid being called a complete orphan.

When Abu disappointedly returned to the hospital, he was surprisingly shocked to see his mother receiving blood. He burst into tears of happiness. His joy was manifested by an inevitable smile. Without a word yet to his mother, Abu rushed to thank the nursing sister in-charge of the ward. He met face to face with Sofa who was also furiously rushing there with a complaint.

When Sofa came back to the hospital after escorting her husband, she expected to see her sister Martina receiving blood. To her greatest surprise, it was Sima receiving it instead. Sofa swelled up with furry, had ran to ask why her sister was not receiving the blood. Coincidentally, while Abu was busy thanking the ward sister for the God-sent blood to his dear old mother, Sofa was there pouring out her grievances concerning her sister's case.

The ward sister was at loss. She remembered Sofa's husband whose blood group fitted Martina's requirement, but what was she hearing? Mother Sima receiving blood when none of her relatives came up with a marching blood group to hers! She was greatly shocked and very afraid that a mistake must have been made. She soon confirmed her thought. Surely the blood meant for Sofa's sister, Martina, was being given to old mother Sima instead. What a dangerous mistake!!!

# CHAPTER TWO

## THE REPERCUSSIONS

THE WARD ATTENDANT felt like melting into thin air. It was all her fault; she took Sima's bed-head ticket to the lab instead of Martina's. She thought she was doing a favour to old mother Sima. She hated Martina because of Sofa's bad atittude. It was a very serious mistake. Sofa, was a rude and quarrelsome woman but Abu has been very good to her. Whenever Abu went out in search of blood donors, he always came back with some gifts for that ward attendant. The reason for such intimacy between Abu and the ward attendant was best known to them. She once overheard the doctors' emphasis on the critical need of blood for Abu's mother. She tearfully pitied her and since then, she had been looking for any slightest chance to help the old woman. Ignorantly, she thought all blood are the same. She was at the laboratory when the blood of Sofa's husband was tested and found to match his sister inlaw's blood group. As a result, the man was instructed to go and take some food to get himself ready for the blood donation. The ward attendant felt the golden opportunity had finally come. She knew the lab technicians would work on any bed-head ticket taken to them from the ward. They would assume it has been sent by the nurse incharge of the affected ward. She was completely ignorant of the final consequences of her plans. She however took advantage of the fact that the ward sister was busy reconciling the account for the day. When the blood was ready, she foolishly acted without enquiries. Her actions led to the dangerous mistake with chains of repercussions. Counting revenue was not very important at that material time. The ward sister in charge knew the whole blame would be on her. Negligence of duty would be the charge against her. The priority line must be shifted towards correcting the wrong without further delay. She immediately opened the table drawer; poured the bunches of Naira notes into it; hurriedly rose up and rushed to the ward. She didn't lock the drawer. The total sum of money left in the drawer was six hundred and fifty Naira. That was a very large sum of money in those days, capable of buying two saloon cars.

The ward sister was unaware that her movements were being monitored. She rushed off, not caring that one patient's relative was curiously watching her. He was called Murvi, the pick-pocket. Amazingly, he saw how carelessly the ward sister left the table drawer unlocked, with a bunch of keys hanging by the key hole. The professional pick-pocket had an urge to attempt something, but he resisted it. He cautioned himself never to take such risks that are too open.

As if in answer to Murvi's prayers, suddenly there was a power failure. The whole ward was immediately thrown into complete darkness. It made things worst for the ward workers who were already in confusion. The ward sister and all the other nurses in the ward, were forced to stand still. Before the light went off, they were busy working on the transfusion of the remaining blood to Martina. The ward attendants were running here and there in the dark looking for matches and bush lamps to be lighted. In their confused state, they even forgot the usual place where lanterns and matches were kept.

Halleluya! Murvi swiftly took advantage of the darkness to fulfill his mission. He silently dashed to the table like a cat jumping to catch a rat. He quickly emptied the whole content of the drawer into his big side pocket. Tactfully he left the drawer well locked and swiftly removed the keys. Moving away with the keys in his hand, Murvi disappeared before the bush lamps were lighted up.

Immediately the bush lamps were lighted, the ward sister picked up one of them. She rushed to her worktable. A slight fearful thought had gripped her mind during the darkness. She was not quiet sure whether or not the drawer was locked when she hurried off to the ward. Her fearful mind was greatly relieved when she confirmed that the drawer was properly locked. She happily moved back to the ward to finish clearing the mess. Unfortunately, she was too busy and confused to care for where the keys were at such a busy moment. All her concern then was how to quickly transfuse the blood to Martina. She was hopelessly praying that there should be no further complications.

Abu was left in a fix. He wondered why his mother was given the blood in the first place. He was not happy. His face automatically changed from the usually jovial and smiling appearance, to a very long, sad and angry one. He peeped at his mother's bed head ticket and read the particulars on it which corresponded to those on the blood bag. Abu felt cheated.

"The blood was really meant for my poor old mother" Abu remarked. He tried to argue against the steps being taken to transfer the blood from his mother to Martina, but nobody cared about him. Every one was very busy doing one thing or the other, all geared towards the blood transfusion. The ward nurses took turns in trying to trace the suitable vein on Martina's arms. The ward attendants were running here and there obeying instructions and doing one thing or the other. Though the night was cold, all the workers were sweating.

Receiving no response to his arguments, Abu had to give

up but said,. "My only hope for explanation is Dr. Mali" he whispered to himself. "I know the Dr. has a special concern for my mother. He will surely explain things to me when he comes." Abu was obliged to wait patiently.

Sofa was a tall slender woman, light in complexion. She always wore a proud look, and could easily be provoked. She hardly controlled her mouth when provoked. 'Barking like a dog' was a common description of the way she talked whenever she becomes angry.

The ward sister was surprised that Sofa had not yet uttered any harsh word following the blood transfusion mistake. She must take precaution to approach her with a word of apology before she became fully charged up. She then called Sofa to an empty corner of the ward. She apologetically explained to her the how and why the mistake. Even though Sofa was at a boiling point, she pretended to understand. Surprisingly, she remained mute, without uttering even a word. They were still standing at the lonely corner when suddenly their attention was drawn towards Sima's bed.

Unfortunately, the blood which was mistakenly given was not of her blood group. Sima's body had started reacting seriously to the foreign blood. All the ward staff were rushing towards Sima's bed. The ward sister abruptly stop her one sided conversation to Sofa. She also rushed to the centre of attraction.

When Abu saw how his mother was developing very heavy lumps all over her body, he thought that was her end. He quietly bent over his knees and started weeping bitterly. Heavy droplets of tears were watering the floor as he wept.

The ward sister straight away ordered for some antihistamine drugs. She started pumping doses into Sima's body. She was panic stricken.

"Oh! God, what does this mean" the ward sister was wondering . She began sweating profusely with absent mindedness. She was contemplating on the consequences of the mistake. First, it was her duty to check the bed-head ticket before allowing it to be taken to the laboratory.

Secondly, she wondered what would happen if Sima's reaction to the blood got worse. Furthermore, she didn't know what explanation to give, since the doctor had already booked Sima for operation the following day.

"The doctor will definitely expect Sima prepared for operation tomorrow". She whispered to herself. After a very long contemplation, the ward sister cooked up a defence.

"I will explain that the patient un-usually reacted to the blood and it was dis-connected straight away to avoid further complications". She concluded. "Yes that is the only probable way out". She said. "It is a bright idea as long as the doctor will only enquire from me alone, but what of if-if-if -----?" She stammered. "Oh God! What of what?" She burst into a shout. She was ignorant of the fact that she had betrayed herself. The patients in the ward and all the other staff simultaneously looked towards her in surprise.

"I am sorry please" she childishly pleaded while trying to force out a smile. "I was carried away by the thoughts of all these happenings, so much so that my thoughts burst into words"

Her shout stimulated Abu who rose swiftly from his croaked weeping position. He sat erect with fearfully bulging eyes. His temperature shot up. His heartbeat suddenly tripled its normal rate. Abu thought the worse had happened. He quickly looked at his old mother and saw her still breathing.

"Why can't you call the doctor"? Abu asked. He was ignorant of the fact that the doctor was the least wanted at that moment. The ward sister was too confused and totally absent minded to withstand and answer any question from a doctor. "There is no cause for alarm, Abu". She gently replied to Abu's question. "Your mother will soon be better. The rashes will subside. There is no use disturbing the doctor over every minor issue". She cautioned.

"But is it a minor issue to transfuse the blood meant for my poor mother to another patient?" Abu sharply replied. He thought it was the removal of the blood from his mother that led to her developing a new problem. His question triggered a grip of painful fear drifting through the ward sisters' heart. If Abu takes a drastic step, she will be in for it.

"We are sorry for that Abu" she said. "It was really a painful mistake. You can bear us witness that none of your relatives came up with blood that matches that of your mother. The blood that your mother was mistakenly given was donated by that woman's husband (pointing to Sofa). He donated the blood for his sister in- law onto whom the blood is being transfused now."

Sofa had so far suppressed her anger, but she couldn't stand it anymore. She overheard the dialogue between Abu and the ward sister. Failing to control herself, Sofa rose up and flared up at Abu. She approached him with an angrily tightened face and clenched teeth.

"Did you say the blood meant for your mother was transfused to another patient?" She asked furiously "Say it again you idiot. If you loved your mother very much, why didn't you go to face the painful needles to give her your blood? You are a coward. Don't let me say it was a connivation between you coward and these old harlots in uniform. You stole my husband's blood for your mother." Sofa continued raining abuses to Abu and the ward staff. "And yet they called themselves trained nursing sisters. God forbid that I should have a sister like any of them".

Sofa was pouring these abuses while drawing close and closer to Abu, pointing her finger straight into his mouth. It got to a point when Abu couldn't bear her insults any longer. He couldn't swallow any more without re-acting. He swiftly rose up and gave her a very heavy slap in the face. She was sent staggering backward and finally landed flat on her back. Instantly, the ward was thrown into a moment of deep silence. As she fell, Sofa forgot to close her mouth which was left open for sometime, but not talking. After about two minutes, Sofa closed her mouth, but still lay quietly on the cold cement floor. She felt her head aching.

Apart from the ward sister incharge, none of the ward staff pitied her. Majority of the patients in the ward were in support of her argument, but none of them could offer any help.

The ward sister incharge only pitied Sofa and wanted to render help, because she didn't want anything to go beyond the walls of the ward. She hated anything of that sort getting into the ears of higher authorities or the police. She begged the ward attendants to carry Sofa to one of the empty beds for better comfort and rest. They reluctantly obeyed, but before they bent down to touch her, she came back to her full senses.

She stood up on her own and quietly moved to Martina's bedside. After sitting down carefully she shamefully looked round without a word.

"I am sorry that I couldn't help you sister" Martina said with a very low sick voice. "You are suffering all these, just for my sake. Why did you go that far? Don't you know the cruelty and hatred of this horrible world? Just see how that man wanted to kill you for nothing"

Some of the ward staff, especially the female ward atten-

dants were mockingly chuckling themselves with laughter behind the doors and ward cupboards. These objects acted as
shields to cover their actions from the ward sister incharge.
They dared not laugh openly to the hearing of the ward sister.
She was eying them with bulging annoyance. She feared that
the laughter could stimulate another trouble.

Abu smilingly walked over to Sofa and said, "Do you still
have more to say with your big mouth? My right hand is jealous of my left hand for doing the quietening job. It is ready for
action too, if you are not yet satisfied". Abu teased, but Sofa
maintained her silence. "You women, sometimes forget that
you have been destined to be weak but you let your mouths
grow very big with dangerous words".

Surprisingly, Abu who was thought to be an illiterate,
proved to all that he knew what he was doing or saying. He
picked up his mother's bed head ticket, read the particulars to
all around; comparing it to the particulars on the blood bag
which was then hanging over Martina. "You can see clearly
here that the blood was meant for my mother. Yet, that old
mother of a drake was bold and brave enough to quarrel with
me for my complaint. Who knows what became of the blood
donated by her so-called husband". Turning to Sofa, he said,
"Let me tell you woman, I will not let this go by. I must seek
and fight for my right".

All these utterances from Abu pricked the ward sister like a
hot needle piercing into a fresh wound. She wondered whether
Abu was going to take the case to the court, the police or what
actually was in his mind? If Abu decided to take the case to
the hospital authorities, she still had a hard nut to crack. She
knew the principal medical officer compromises to no silly
mistakes. She made a move to stop Abu from talking more,
but she was afraid of calling for a similar action from Abu,

as was received by Sofa. She was too weak and exhausted to stand Abu's slap. The time was running towards the end of their duty period. She would soon hand over and rest.

# CHAPTER THREE

# THE HANDING OVER PROCESS

IT WAS ALREADY 9.00PM. The night duty staff had arrived to take over from the evening shift. Sentoria the nursing sister to take over the female ward had also arrived. She was surprised to meet her colleague in a disorderly manner. She saw her absent-mindedly bending over one of the patient's bed, seeming to be in a very deep agonistic thought.

"What is wrong sister" Sentoria asked at last. She shoke her. Fibina slowly lifted her head up. Upon seeing sister Sentoria, she remembered that her duty time was over. She had to hand over at last. That was the long awaited moment

"What is wrong sister?" Sentoria repeated her question. "You seemed to have been struck with a sudden sickness".

"Oh! So you have already come, Sento?" Fibena replied, trying hard to put on a smiling face. "Iam exhausted. Iam glad that you have come at last. Infact, we had a very busy and hectic duty today"

The two sisters, straight away moved to the staff's room to start the handing over process. A strip of fear ran through Fibina's spinal cord. For the first time she thought of the drawer's keys. The revenue collectors receipts which she forgot to lock up, were still found scattered on the table. Sentoria helped her to pack the security books into the heaps of used up (4); in use (1) and un-used (5). This came up to ten (10) receipt booklets to be handed over. The only receipt booklet which was still in use, recorded a total of six hundred and fifty Naira (N650.00) revenue collected during Fibina's shift.

"This is by far the highest revenue collected in one shift in our hospital". Sentoria commented. Fibina couldn't respond. She was busy ransacking the other items on the table, looking for the drawer's keys.

"Oh! God, What are all these?" Fibina uttered in great panic. "I am sure they were here but where could they be now?"

"Go gently Fibi" Sentoria Cautioned. "You must have just misplaced them, and if you do things in a hurry, you might never find them".

"Infact, today is the worst day in my life. I pray that history would not repeat itself. I pray that the ghost of my parents, should guide me from making such silly mistakes anymore".

Fibina had lost both her parents in a ghastly motor accident when she was still only ten years old. She grew up with the belief that the ghost of dead relatives could guide one against misfortunes. The story of how her parents died was narrated to her by her uncle Kebi.

They had gone to attend Kebi's wedding ceremony. Fibina's father who was Kebi's elder brother had gotten himself totally drunk during the celebration. At last, he insisted to drive home that same night. Kebi tried all he could to stop him, but to no avail. Even Fibina's mother was against their going home that night. However, She had to undertake the risk. She didn't want to leave the husband to drive home alone.

Fibina was one of the flower girls. She was highly favoured by the bride. Their tradition holds that any child in the clan favoured by the new wife, will be allowed to keep her company for four days. This explained why Fibina did not follow her parents home.

Fibina's father drove off nicely at first, but soon after, the car started swaying from one side of the road to the other. Half dozing and half awake, the drunken man drove on. He was now to negotiate a corner. He didn't notice an oncoming big lorry. Trying to negotiate the corner, he went off his own lane. Unfortunately, the lorry was negotiating the same bend and because the car was now on its lane, they met face to face. The big lorry ran over the small vehicle, flattening it completely together with its occupants. That was how Fibina became an orphan just overnight. Let us go back to the handing over process. "What do you mean Fibi?"

Sentoria asked, "Had anything gone wrong before apart from the keys being looked for?"

"Nothing sister" Fibina replied not willing to go into details. "It is only that I had misplaced the keys. I am really very tired. I want to handover and go home. That's all".

"It's a pity sister" Sentoria sympathized with her. "Where could they have gone? Are you sure you had them when you were finally leaving for the ward?"

"Yes, I made sure the drawer was properly locked as you can see here by your self. I removed the keys and pocketed them" she lied.

Sentoria bent over; touch the drawer and attempted pulling it out to confirm that it was locked.

"It is really locked, but where could the keys be?" Sentoria concluded. "Shall we continue to waste time looking for the keys?".

"No, sister" Fibina answered .I suggest we go on with other aspects of the hand over, before coming back to financial matters". Fibina had very slight hope of finding the keys later. She was really not sure of where the keys could be. She was seriously doubting whether or not she actually locked the drawer personally. It could have been locked by one good or bad Samaritan. Her body Started shaking vigorously in great panic once more. As before, she started sweating, despite the cold night. Luckily for her, the ward bush lamp was dim. A brighter light could have exposed all these fearful signs manifested. Sister Sentoria and her group could have wondered what was actually wrong with Fibina that night.

Sister Fibna was the only evening shift staff left. She had released all her other staff at nine to go home. It was already 9.30PM and yet the handing over process was still at a scratch.

Un-expectedly and against the will of sister Fibina, the electric light flushed in. Its brightness led to the exposition of all secrets that hitherto lay hidden behind the partial darkness. Sister Fibina had no time and place to hide her face. Awfully, the face was fear stricken with droplets of sweat. In the absence of a handkerchief, she suddenly pulled up one edge of her white uniform and started wiping her face with it. That portion of the uniform was conspicuously left stained.

"Why is she sweating that much with suspiciously fearful looks" Adini whispered to Kimba. Both of them were ward attendants. They came in together wither Sentoria to take over from the evening duty staff. They were peeping at the two nursing sisters from behind one big ward cupboard.

"Don't you know that old mother of a cheat?". Kimba replied "who knows whether or not she actually put the said amount of money in the drawer? She is now pretending that the drawer keys are lost"

That was said by Kimba who was one day seriously punished by sister Fibina for mis-behaving. Kimba and sister Fibina happened to be on the same shift that day. Kimba had acted cruelly to a female patient who was in critical condition and Sister Fibina made Kimba to wash the ward toilet alone that morning. Since then, Kimba hated Fibina and never saw anything good about that Nursing Sister. The female patient in question had just undergone D & C. She was bleeding and though the patient tried her best to avoid soiling her beddings, some blood mistakenly touched one of the white bed sheets, on her bed. On admission, the patient was asked to provide four bars of soap and two packets of omo. These items were to be used for washing patient's hospital clothes and beddings. She had fulfilled all the requirements.

That fateful morning, Kimba was gathering the ward beddings for washing. When she came to the bed of the patient in question, she saw the blood stained bedsheet. She was not happy. She decided to pick up that bed sheet separately. With the bed sheet in hand, she went round looking for that patient. She found her sitting outside the ward, charting with her husband. The poor sick woman was holding a bowl filled with gruel, she was sipping it as they charted. Kimba went straight to the patient and without a word of excuse, she flung the stained bed sheet unto the patient's face. Unfortunately, one of the edges of the bedsheet went into her bowl of gruel.

"This is your bedsheet, You careless and filty woman" Kimba said with angry twisted face. "If every patient were to paint their bed sheet red with blood, do you think you could have anyone clean to sleep on? Take and wash it yourself as a lesson to be careful next time".

The patient and her husband were highly embarrassed. The hungry patient who had spent the night without food, had no alternative, but to pour her gruel away. Her husband was stricken dumb in surprise. He felt highly touched by such an inhuman behaviour of the ward attendant. At last he took the case to sister Fibina who had to punish Kimba.

Sister Fibina and Sentoria proceeded to the ward. They got to Sima's bed.

"This is the patient who was due to receive blood" Fibina said, pointing to Sima. "She however reacted to it and the transfusion process was stopped immediately". The two nursing sisters proceeded to Martina's bed.

"This patient will go for operation tomorrow. The blood which she is receiving was donated by her sister's husband. Just then, Sofa looked up exposing her big swollen mouth.The slap Abu gave her was too hard. The heat generated, provided extra energy for faster cell multiplication at the embark site. The swollen mouth had disfigured Sofa greatly. The usual beautiful round faced lady, then looked like an ugly ape. Fibina was not ready for questions, but before she turned to the next bed, Sentoria shot her with one.

"What happened to Martina's sister? Was she involved in an accident? Her mouth seems to have been freshly hurt".

"Yes, it was an accident. She had a mis-understanding with one other patient's relative". Fibina answered reluctantly while walking away.

"A mis-understanding? Over what?" Sentoria asked with no hope of getting an answer.

"If you don't mind, let us get going please". Fibina pleaded. "I told you that I am both tired and exhausted. Can't you just pity me?" Fibina felt like crying.

"Oh! Sister,I actually sympathize with you, but just make one thing clear to me please". Sentoria continuously pleaded. "I have observed one thing which obviously needs clarification". Sentoria was gazing at the blood bag hanging over Martina. Fibina's heart went into pieces. She knew Sentoria wouldn't miss it. She was very observant and tactful in her work. No trap set for her will ever make an easy catch. Sometimes Fibina admired Sentoria's style of duty, but she is usually jealous of her exceptional brilliance. Fibina had guessed rightly. Sentoria had seen the blood bag hanging over Martina, bearing the paticulars of mother Sima.

"I think there was a mistake sister" Sentoria observed. "This blood bag has the particulars of that old woman over there. It puzzles me to see this woman called Martina receiving the blood instead. Why is it so?"

"I will explain that later please" Fibina pleadingly requested. "Let us go on to other more important issues for now, if you don't mind." Their discussions were being monitored by the two ward attendants. They had enough grounds for their dangerous gossip against Fibina.

# CHAPTER FOUR

# DANGEROUS GOSSIP

THE TWO FEMALE WARD ATTENDANTS, Kimba and Adini, were alert to all the conservations of the two nursing sisters during the handing over process. They were paying more attention to what transpired between the two ward sisters instead of concentrating on their duty. Kimba was more critically attentive than Adini.

"Didn't I tell you that she is a devil in all ways?" Kimba whispered to Adini. "The other time, it was the case of the government revenue that should be suspended. The drawer's keys cannot be traced. Now it is a case of blood meant for one patient, but being given to another one. You must have also heard that the explanation for this, is to be suspended too".

"Yes, I overheard that" Adini concorded.

"Who knows, it is possible that before the handing over process ends, they may come across a case of a dead patient to be suspended or rather, its explanations to be made later."

"Haba Kimba!, you are going too far" Adini said. "You don't seem to like sister Fibina at all. Don't you think you could be castigating her innocently?"

"You don't know what that daughter of a bitch did to me, Adini. You don't know her because you are just newly posted to this ward. You will tell me one day, when you happen to come on the same shift with her" Kimba said.

"What did she do Kimba?"

"She is just born cruel my sister. She has cruelty in her

blood, nerves, saliva and all over her body".

"What really happened, Kimba?"

"You know that old bucket system toilet behind this ward, don't you?"

"Yes I know. I hate the place. Even flies will hate to visit it especially early in the mornings"

"You are perfectly right."

It is usually full of many varieties of human products. The floor is always completely covered with lumps of the stuff. One hardly sees the hole leading into the bucket"

"I feel like vomiting"

"Believe me Adini. One early morning, that cruel devil made me to wash that toilet thoroughly clean and all alone".

"You are not serious, Kimba" Adini doubtedly commented. "What was really the crime you committed?"

"I didn't do anything wrong" Kimba replied. "This is a true story my sister. Now that you are in this ward, Iam sure you will soon come on the same shift with her. My ears are open to hear a worst story about her from you one day."

"Please tell me about your encounter with her first. I am anxious to hear Kimba."

"It was just because she met me one morning advising one patient not to be careless with her beddings. That monkey felt it was enough reason to earn me a prisoner's punishment" "A prisoner's punishment indeed" Adini concorded. "But Kimba, please tell me, did you do it?"

"What do you mean?"

"I mean carrying out the punishment".

"Who am I not to do it my sister? Don't you know that she has the command of the Principal Nursing Officer (PNO)? Who else could I have cried to, considering our helpless position in the society? You know by then, the bell of retrenchment was ringing loud and clear into the ears of everyworker. I would have been committing a multi-suicide if I dis-obeyed the so-called seniors. The lives of my five poor children and my self could have been in danger. What a risk, if I dared to refuse doing it!"

"Is your husband not earning any income to support the family?"

"My husband is a poor carpenter. Since inflation captured our country, he has never used his tools for the past eight months. Unlike the good old days, there are no more roofs and ceilings, to make. People seem to have resigned from building new houses. Nobody seem to be repairing the old dilapidating ones that usually needed the services of carpenters. He doesn't even make new chairs or tables as before due to lack of capital to buy timbers and planks. Apart from these, prices of nails have gone beyond the reach of common men like him. Nobody seem to be repairing damaged doors, broken windows, chairs, tables and stools, any more. Even children who were usually the cause of all these damages, seem to have resigned from their jobs. Their resignations coupled with the hard bite of inflation, have rendered my husband redundant. My husband had been forced to go on compulsory retirement from his self-employment without benefit." Kimba continued talking without end. She was trying to explain in detail why she had to accept the brutal punishment. She wanted Adini to see with her, that there was no way out. She was the only breadwinner for the family. She seriously blamed the inflation for turning her husband from active service to idle service.

On the other side, Sentoria and Fibina were pushing on with the handing over process.The two nursing sisters had gone round to all the patients in the ward. They were back to the staff 's room. The drawer's key was not yet found.

"I suggest we force the drawer open" Sentoria said

"What of the money?"

"You could take it home and bring it back tomorrow. It would not be safe to keep the money here, if the drawer's lock is destroyed"

"It is equally risky traveling home with such a large sum of money at a very late hour like this" Fibina replied. "However, taking it home as you said, seemed to be a brighter and safer idea. Let us call the compound nurse to hear his own view."

The two ward attendants, Kimba and Adini were sent to call the compound nurse. The compound office was situated at the far end of a long corridor linking all the wards. The two attendants felt greatly relieved. They left the ward immediately. They were happy that they could then talk freely, no more in whispers.

"I knew that crook will support the idea of taking the money home" Kimba said as soon as they were out of the ward.

"Why did you say so?"

"It is said that she operates a private business where she pumps in government money for her personal gain"

"Are you sure?"

"I am not quite sure, but I was told by one woman. I believe that woman can not tell a lie."

"Now that the eye of the government is sharp and wide open to catch dubious workers, I would be surprised if your allegation were true."

"My sister, let us not rule out that possibility completely. Devils like sister Fibina could do a lot, even in the face of danger. I highly support the government for launching the 'War Against Indiscipline (WAI).'

"Why"

"Because we now know those who are in discipline. All

those affected, usually wear the 'WAI' badge. Wearing the badge means an open confession of an inner guilt of indiscipline. The badge indicates that the owner is indiscipline and there is a serious war against it in him or her. You know sister Fibina always wears the badge. She knows that she is indiscipline. The number of those wearing the badges are many in this country. Uncountable number of people are really fighting the war in this our great nation. I wish all the fighters victory. Let them conquer the indiscipline they harbour. At the end of the war, I pray that each of them would tell the world the result of their fights. Let them tell us the number and types of indiscipline each of them had been able to overcome, capture and killed" Kimba monopolized the conversation again. Adini was left completely speechless.

"Some of the indiscipline could escape the fight and hide, only to emerge after the war." Adini managed to come in.

"If that happens, I will be glad if sister Fibina will count cruelty as one of those she captured and killed." The two attendants burst into laughter.

The gossip conversation was too sweet that the two attendants missed their way. They had passed the compound office and were instead heading towards doctor Mali's consulting room, the doctor was on call that night. He had told the hospital staff never to go to his house for calls. They were to go straight to the consulting room where he prefers to wait for all calls. He heard their footsteps and some voices approaching his room. The footsteps and voices grew loud and louder. He was very attentive. He recognized Kimba's voice. He overheard the conversation of the two attendants. Not all, but the last portion. He clearly heard the portion which said, "sister Fibina always wears the badge. She knows that she is indiscipline ................." to "I will be glad if sister Fibina will count cruelty as one of those she captured and killed." The doctor nodded his head and waited.

Timbo Hospital was badly noted for junior staff gossiping against the senior ones. Consequently, an official circular was issued with very strong warning. The circular also stated that anyone caught committing such an offence will be dismissed on the sport.

There was a knock at the door. The doctor answered. It was only then that the two attendants realized with a shock that they were in the wrong place.

The doctor's voice was quite clear and distinct from that of the compound nurse. They were in for it. They knew doctor Mali was good at catching conversations. Their minds reflected to the serious gossip circular.

"Oh! God! Help me" Kimba exclaimed prayerfully. "This surely implies my work is at stake. Fibina's gods are at my neck"

The two attendants shockingly hesitated at the door for about five minutes. At last, they had to enter as the doctor opened the door for them.

# CHAPTER FIVE

# AT DOCTOR MALI'S CONSULTING ROOM

"GOOD EVENING DOCTOR" Adini greeted. "We are on our way to the compound nurse, but we felt like calling to say hello" she lied. Adini was still a new employee. She didn't know exactly where the compound office was compared to the doctor's room. The lie she fabricated, made things worst for Kimba. Kimba knew the doctor was aware that they had missed their way. He knew that Adini was lying. No, both of them were lying since Adini was speaking on their behalf.

Kimba had received his last warning for gossiping. Now she was caught red handed by one of the senior staff in the hospital. Caught gossiping against a Senior staff again and Adini had dragged her into another offence of lying to the doctor. She must defend herself against this before it gets too late.

"We actually missed our way doctor." Kimba confessed, while forcing a pale smile through her fear stricken face.

"I knew you missed your way even before you said it". The doctor interrupted her with a true smile in return. "Any way before you leave, may I know the source of your conversations, please?"

Kimba's hairs rose to ends. She took a deep breath in and forced it out with a question. "What conversation doctor?" She said pretending to be sober.

"Those gossips which drove your heads from the right

to the wrong place .Are you not aware of the recent circular against gossips?"

Kimba was already far away in thought. She was imagining what would happen if she were dismissed. She estimated that her one hundred Naira saving, would last only for about five weeks. She may enjoy the favour of her relatives and neighbours for another one week. At last, she and her family will be in for the worst. She recalled all the pieces of advice her old mother used to give her. She regretted her rejection of the advice that she should invest in farming. "Now, I realize that farming is very important" Kimba remembered the hoe which her old mother had given her. She had left it rusting away behind the house. She had never given a damn to the government's "Operation Go back to Land" until that very moment. Kimba's reverie lasted for about thirty seconds.

On the other hand, Adini was battling with the shame of openly lying to the doctor. She felt like eating Kimba raw for conflicting her defence before the doctor. "Now I am a liar and yet this is my first contact with the doctor. Oh! What a disgrace!" Adini started thinking deeply as well.

"Kimba is cruel. She is as cruel as sister Fibina. Why did she exonerate herself by confessing that we missed our way to the doctor, when I said it was willful? I must blame myself too. I was too fast to speak. I should have given Kimba the opportunity to speak as my senior. Whatever she said, I wouldn't have dared to go against her statements. I think my head is aching. I am sick. I was stupid. No, I think we were both stupid" The doctor gave the two attendants enough time to battle with their thoughts. At last he broke the silence.

"O.K, let me have the answer to my question please". The two attendants were still silent. The doctor looked eagerly at them. Inwardly he had a special attraction for Kimba. That feeling has always been there whenever he met Kimba, but he had never expressed it. "Both of you are not speaking, isn't it?" the doctor shouted at them. "However, Adini you can go ahead to call the compound nurse for your ward sister. Kimba will follow you after answering my question"

"But I am not supposed to move about alone at this late hour of the night doctor" Adini complained.

"You are right. Kimba should escort you to the compound nurse. After calling him, both of you will escort her back to my room. From here you and the compound nurse will proceed to the ward".

The two attendants rushed out of the doctor's room as if being driven by a mad dog. They felt greatly relieved. They were going to talk over their differences, but it will have to be in whispers. They dared not speak aloud anymore. They controlled their temper until they were off from the doctor's room.

"You were too fast Adini" Kimba said at last. "You don't know Dr. Mali. He is too cunny to be deceived"

"Is that why you introduced me as a liar to him?"

"I am sorry Adini. I really understand what you mean, but I was forced to jump in with the truth. That is the only defence he accommodates. Lies have no place in his blood. There is no use going to the warfront with a toy gun."

"I am also sorry Kimba, I now understand. Lets get going. Hope we are now on the right path?"

"Yes my sister. No more mistakes. Here is the compound office" Kimba knocked at the door.

"Come in" the compound nurse answered. The two attendants went in and greeted. They explained their mission to him and also told him about the doctor's directives. He left with them immediately. Mr. Kingsbay the compound nurse was a friend to Adini's husband. He was a green snake in a green grass. Whenever he visited them at home or when he meets Adini in the hospital, he had always suppressed the urge to openly show his love to her. After escorting Kimba to doctor Mali's room, Kingsbay lured Adini back to the compound office. Sister Fibina and Sentoria were kept waiting. The handing over process came to a stand still pending the arrival of the compound nurse.

# CHAPTER SIX

# HOW KINGSBAY AND ADINI'S HUSBAND BECAME FRIENDS

ADINI WAS A FAIR LOOKING BEAUTIFUL WOMAN. She got married, not long ago to a young member of the state criminal investigation department (CID). Her husband was very good at his work. His friend Kingsbay has never suspected him to be a member of the state CID, despite their long stay together.

The story of how they became friends was funny. Adini's husband, frequently visited beer parlours and hotels. He went to those places, not to get himself drunk, nor for chasing loose women. It was part of his official duties to cover such areas. It was in one of such places that he met Kingsbay for the first time. One funny thing was that nobody had ever seen Mr. Cunny the CID member drinking more than one bottle of beer at a sitting. The fact is that Mr. Cunny had never taken more than one bottle per day but he was always seen drunk. His nature of duty requires him to be sober upstairs, but an outwardly complete drunkard to the world, especially his targets.

Most of his targets drank beer. That was why Mr. Cunny usually used the beer parlours as theatre rooms for operating them. If he happened to get to a hotel earlier than his targets, he only waited for them without drinking. Immediately he noticed their arrival, he pretentiously became too drunk to take anymore than one bottle. If those he had targeted happened to have gone to a hotel earlier than him, Mr. Cunny would pretentiously come in too drunk to take anymore than one bottle of beer. He was very dedicated and hard working. Mr. Cunny always had enough official money to play about with during his duty. Surprisingly, he had never cheated the government at all. He had honesty ingrained in his blood. He never bought beer for innocent citizens. Those under suspicion or investigations for criminal cases usually enjoyed more drinks from him. His secretary at work was a wristwatch which was also a devise for tape recording. After he had lured his targets into friendship and drunkenness, he had no problem in squeezing out all the truth from them. That was how he succeeded in drawing Mr. Kingsbay to the police station for siphoning drugs from Timbo hospital into his private business. Unbelievably, this action however brought them into tight friendship.

Serious allegations had reached the state CID headquarters that drugs were disappearing fast from Timbo hospital. It was alleged that some senior hospital staff were responsible for draining the drugs away for their personal benefits. Mr. Cunny was assigned to handle the issue.

One after the other, Mr. Cunny tactifully combed and screened all the senior staff of Timbo hospital. He found all of them innocent except Mr. Kingsbay who was yet to be investigated. None of those who went through Mr. Cunny's investigation exercise, ever knew that they were being screened.

Mr. Cunny tactfully got to know that Mr. Kingsbay used to spend most of his evenings in Timbo central hotel (TCH). He knew Mr. Kingsbay goes to that hotel at about five o'clock in the evening. Mr. Cunny scheduled to meet him there.

One evening, the CID member left his house at about quarter to five. As usual, he was riding one old bicycle towards Timbo central hotel. From the way Mr. Cunny behaved in beer parlours and the way he rode his old bicycle, those who knew him, nick-named him Mr. D, meaning drunkard or V.H meaning Village Headmaster. From far, he saw a white beetle car packed by the road side. As he drew near the car he recognized it as Kingsbay's own. Somebody was in the car and that must be Kingsbay himself. He knew the owner of the car was on his way to the central hotel. Only God knew why he had to stop and pack by the roadside.

Immediately Mr. Cunny saw his target ahead of him, he automatically changed his style of riding to reflect a drunken rider. He wore a tattered pair of trouser and a very old shirt torn at the back .He passed by the car, riding like a typical drunken fellow.

"That man must have drunk his head off somewhere". Kingsbay commented. He saw how the bicycle was swaying from one side to the other with very little control. "These are the type of people who could easily draw one into very serious trouble if one doesn't drive carefully. They easily cause accident on the high way". Kingsbay was quarrelling alone in his car.

Mr. Cunny got to the hotel ten minutes earlier than Kingsbay. Just enough time to order for one bottle of beer as usual. He asked for one small thumbler, filled the glass cup and swallowed its content. That was enough to give his mouth some smell of beer. He selected one empty table by the corner where he got himself seated. He bent over the table and pretended to be dozing off. All his attentions were centred at the door to catch Kingsbay's arrival. It wasn't long when Mr. Kingsbay came into the hotel. Just simultaneously, Mr. Cunny tactfully sat up erect and was the first to wave him to a chair by his side.

"Please kindly sit down here and keep me company Mr.Kingsbay. You may not know me, but I know you. Are you not the compound nurse at Timbo hospital?"

"Yes, but how did you know me?"

"You were kind to my brother today. Your kindness really saved his life".

"What did I really do please?"

"The drugs you gave him, really worked wonders. I will never forget you for that. Please sit down and let me offer you one". Mr Cunny said with a drunken look and actions typical of drunkards.

Mr. Kingsbay was greatly puzzled, wondering how Mr. Cunny knew him even by name, but he soon felt it was typical of some good patient relatives. They were usually appreciative of any little favour shown to them. He wanted to refuse sitting down, but the offer of one bottle from Mr. Cunny, made him to take the seat. As he sat down, Kingsbay said "I am really surprised how you knew me by name? I went to work today, but I can't remember seeing a face like yours there". Kingsbay took a quick look at the counter. He was really thirsty for beer and felt the ordered bottle of beer was being delayed.

"Good people rarely know all those who praise them, mark you Mr. Kingsbay, I said it was my brother you gave the drugs. However, I went with him, but probably you had too many people to remember all. Your goodness has really made you very popular in the hospital. Don't be surprised that many people know you even better than by your name".

Mr. Kingsbay started taking his first bottle of beer. He had the imagination that Mr. Cunny must have taken about five to seven bottles by then. He erroneously based his judgment on Mr. Cunny's look and behaviour. Little did he know that Cunny was an expert actor of drunkenness. He had actually not gone beyond the first glass cup–full taken just before Kingsbay arrived.

After greedily emptying four bottles, three bought by Mr,

Cunny and one bought by himself, Kingsbay became like a ripe field of rice ready for harvest by the C.I.D.

"Sir" Mr. Cunny drew his attention. "I am sorry for talking too much. Please don't take me for a drunk. I have a problem which requires your assistance. Would you kindly allow me to lay it before you please?"

"What problem? I grant you an un-conditional permission to lay it flat". Mr. Kingslay replied with a true drunken tone.

"Thank you sir. I have long had a serious disease which I am ashamed to discuss openly. Now that we are just alone at this corner as new friends, I am glad you offered to help".

"New friends indeed" Kingsbay interrupted. "Since I came to Timbo town, I have never come across someone as kind as you are. I regret I didn't come out with enough money. I would have given you an equal kind treatment with beer, meat etc etc.

"Thank you, just tackle my problem and I will be more than happy.

"I know your disease before you say it" Kingsbay replied. "The process of getting that disease is sweet and joyful, but to get rid of it, brings embracement, shame, pain and sad disgrace in most cases. I will advise you Mr.Cunny to beware of loose women. Apart from draining your pockets, such creatures harbour such dangerous diseases like the one you now suffer from." Mr. Kingsbay was drunkenly carried away by the imagination of a physical disease bothering Cunny.

"I am sorry to have given you wrong impression of my type of disease please. It is not physical and has nothing to do with women please."

"What then is the disease which you are ashamed of, if not STD? Come out clearly please. I will surely try to assist if I can."

# CHAPTER SEVEN

# MR. CUNNY'S NONE PHYSICAL DISEASE

MR.CUNNY SAW THAT HIS NEW FRIEND was drunk enough to be operated on the CID way. He wasted no time but went on to his main mission for the day.

"You are right my friend. Let me hit the nail on the head." Mr. Cunny said.

"Exactly, that is what I want"

"Here we are. I want to start a business in medicine. Since you are already in that field, working in a recognized hospital, I think I am in the right track".

"What do you mean?"

"Actually I want to get in touch with those who have access to free government drugs. I have the money to buy and start the business. I will be grateful if you will connect me to any of the top officers in Timbo hospital. I mean those who will be willing to go into real business with me"

"What did you say?" Kingsbay asked absent-mindedly. "I am sorry Mr. Cunny. I didn't hear you properly because my attention was drawn to that chick over there. Please repeat yourself."

"You seem to have lost interest in our conversation, Mr. Kingsbay."

"No, I am really with you my dear friend. That big bottomed devil has gone out and off from the reach of my attentions. Lets continue please."

"Alright, I was asking if you could connect me to any of your colleagues in the office for business transactions".

"Oh! Yes I now understand. You were talking of business in medicine deals, isn't it?"

"That's correct. Do you know someone I could contact?"

"You are already connected, my friend. The only thing remaining is the deal". Kingsbay said with more and more display of drunkenness.

"What do you mean by the deal, please?"

"I mean how you would like us to carry out the transactions."

"Do you have access to loose drugs?"

"Let me tell you my friend, I am a staff nurse, working in the compound office and at the same time as the hospital pharmacist because right now we have no pharmacist"

Mr. Cunny sensed that his prey was heading straight into his trap. He lured Kingsbay into talking more.

"Infact, my dear, I have long thought of this business, but I didn't know how to go about it. The money to do it is there, but how to do it is my problem. I give you the honour to suggest how we could go about it please."

"How much do you have to start with?"

"I have about two hundred thousand Naira and could secure more if need be"

"My friend, you know this is a serious deal. May I know your correct names before we continue please"

"I am known as Mr. Java Cunny. May I also know your first name please"

"My first name is Kings and my surname is Bay. You already know me as Kingsbay. This connection was made during my school days. My mates refused to call me Kings. To them, the word 'Kings' was highly dignified and superior. They preferred to say I was kings, but bare headed and hence the connection 'Kingsbay'. Since then, I became popularly known as Kingsbay."

"Thank you for that explanation please. I could as well call you Mr. Bay, isn't it?

Yes, but that is not popular".

"Alright, lets keep at Kingsbay and proceed with our business deal please."

"Yes, you are right. Before we go into the deal, it might interest you to know that Timbo hospital gets the largest share of drugs and it covers all kinds." Kingsbay proudly said this to lure Mr. Cunny into making a good offer to him.

"That is marvelous!"

"Yes and we get our supply once every month."

"That is wonderful! How long does each supply last?"

"Not more than one week per chance"

"Surprising! Why so short a time Mr. Kingsbay?"

"Because people like you, who make business with Kingsbay, usually smuggle away over 95% of the drugs. At the end, I would be left alone to sing the usual 'O.S' song to the patients. Some of them even go as far as calling me Mr. 'O.S', meaning out of stock."

"It appears you are already deep in the business with other people. Am I not too late for a big deal?"

"Too late!! You are not. I don't go into such business with anyone who can not give me advance".

"Why"

"Because it is a risky game. The bigger the advance , the better an insurance that my client is serious".

"How much advance do you have already for the next consignment?"

"Right now, I have nobody's advance on me"

"I may be lucky then."

"If you play your card well, I don't mind taking it up with you alone. The fewer people one deals with, the less risk involved."

"How much advance will you require from me please?"

"It depends on the quantity you require"

"That's true. How much of the drugs can you offer me please?"

"Right now we have nothing left in the store."

"You mean everything is now 'O.S'?" Mr. Cunny showed a sign of disappointment.

"Yes, but don't be discouraged. This month's consignment will be coming in tomorrow."

"Thank God. My hope is back in full."

"You can relax properly Mr. Cunny. I will not disappoint you".

"How much of the supply can you spare for me?"

"I still have some small left over drugs from last month's supply. This could take care of our meager issue to the wards for this month. I could therefore spare you the whole consignment for this month, if you could afford to have all"

"Oh! Thank you Mr. Kingsbay. I will be the luckiest fellow".

"Can you afford to buy all?"

"How much will the whole consignment cost please?"

"It will cost only two hundred and fifty thousand Naira."

"Is that not too costly? How much gain could one make at last?"

"I assure you that even if you sell it out at a give away price to wholesale buyers, you will come out with nothing less than eight hundred thousand Naira."

"I am interested and I think I can afford it. How much advance will you require for this please?"

"Only one hundred and fifty thousand Naira. You pay the rest immediately after delivery."

"How shall we go about the transactions of delivery and payments?"

"Simple. Do you have a medicine store?"

"No, not yet. I may still need your advice on how to establish one."

"It seems you are not yet ready to receive the offer I made to you, Mr. Cunny"

"I am quiet ready with the advance, but I really want your advice on how to receive and keep the drugs. You know I am still new in the business."

"How do you think I can help?"

"If you had a store of your own, I can pay you extra amount to receive the drugs for me until I secure my own."

"Actually, I have a store, but it is a double risk to keep such a large quantity of drugs there".

"What of receiving the drugs for me in the hospital store pending when I get a store of mine? I will try not to be long in my arrangements for a store".

"That is impossible. The usual thing is that, immediately the drugs come, the quantity for business will be issued out to the compound nurse. The compound nurse is supposed to distribute to the various wards. Since I am the pharmacist to issue out and at the same time the compound nurse to receive, the store ledgers are always neat. You now know why I can't retain any drugs which I can't account for in the store?."

"How do you usually escape getting caught, Mr. Kingsbay?"

"Its simply the trick of pen and ink. Whoever comes to check, relies on good records and proper signatures. I am good at presenting both very neatly"

"Now Mr. Kingsbay, please help me out. What could be the best way for me to have the drugs?"

"How big is your house Mr. Java?"

"Quiet big. It has three bed rooms and the sitting room".

"Do you use all the rooms?"

"No, we use only two bedrooms and a sitting room."

"What is the size of the empty room?"

"Its about 12ft long, 13ft wide and 9ft from the floor to the ceiling"

"Beautiful. It could comfortably contain the said amount of drugs, packing from the floor to the ceilings"

"My God!" Mr. Cunny exclaimed in his mind. "A big room full of drugs, costing two hundred and five thousand Naira. This is what an individual makes away with." Mr Cunny could not speak for some seconds.

"Why are you silent, Mr. Cunny?" Kingsbay had to ask.

"I was just thinking of other alternatives, but it appears that room is the best."

"I know it will be alright"

"Now how do I give you the advance, please."

# CHAPTER EIGHT

# THE PAYMENT DEAL

"DID YOU SAY you have part of the advance on you here?" Mr. Kingsbay asked.

"Yes, but I feel I should pay you the whole amount of the advance"

"You mean you have that lot sum of money right here on you?"

"Not right here in the hotel please"

"I would have been surprised if you did."

"I can go and bring it from home if you don't mind"

"Why should I mind my friend!"

"Hope you will provide me a receipt on payment."

"That will not be a problem. However, I want you to know that in a business like this, we don't talk much about receipts. I will issue you with it, just because you are still new in the game. It will act as an insurance against the advance payment. When I deliver the goods, you will make the full payment and the receipt should be returned to me".

"Why is it so please?"

"Don't you know this deal is illegal?"

"I am aware"

"You now see why un-necessary documents of proves are not required"

"I now understand. Could I go now to collect the money please? I will go as fast as my horse would take me"

A thought flashed through Mr. Kingsbay that Mr. Cunny

could probably be a C.I.D member. His hairs rose at the ends in fear. He had to make sure Mr. Cunny was not actually a Cunny man. He therefore offered to give him a lift in his Volkswagen beetle car since his bicycle would take him longer time.

"If you don't mind, I offer you the service of my car. Your bicycle could remain here till we come back".

"That's very kind of you, Mr. Kingsbay. Why should I mind? It makes things even faster"

Mr. Kingsbay felt a relief. He thought Mr. Cunny might not be a CID member after all. By the way, business is a risk. Success or failures are either of the two ends.

Kingsbay ignorantly drove his friend to one big CID bungalow in town. They met one young CID woman who acted as the house girl. There was also another member who acted as Mr.Cunny's brother. He pretended as if he had just arrived to see Mr. Cunny for an urgent discussion. However, in the actual sense, he was the treasurer of the secretly marked security notes.

"Please feel free and sit down Mr. Kingsbay" Cunny showed him to one comfortable executive chair. He made the introductions.

"This is my younger brother Ben who has just arrived to see me and this is Mr. Kingsbay, a medical nurse in Timbo hospital".

"Happy to meet you Ben"

"Same to you sir."

Both shook hands and smiled to each other. The female CID member soon appeared from one of the rooms.

"You are welcome, sir" she greeted humbly. "What drinks can I offer you sir?"

"Please entertain my friend: Ben wants to talk to me about

something urgent and private." Mr. Cunny said as he went into the inner room with Ben. Kingsbay was served with a cold beer of his choice.

"That is actually the prey involved in the drug scandal in Timbo hospital, Ben" Mr. Cunny said immediately they were in the inner room.

"How deep is he in for it?"

"He is the hole itself. We 'll talk more later. Right now, I want to sign out one hundred and fifty thousand Naira marked please"

"That's O .K. Here you are cunny" he handed to him the said sum of money from a computerized save. Ben only needed to press some buttons to bring out the amount required.

"Thank you Ben."

"Don't mention. How good is your secretary at its job Cunny?"

"Perfectly well" Mr. Cunny switched on his tape record wristwatch and it intoned the portion "immediately the drugs come, the quantity for business will be issued out to the compound nurse. The compound nurse is supposed to distribute same to the various wards. Since I am the pharmacist to issue out, and at the same time the compound nurse to receive, the store ledgers are always neat."

"You are wonderful, Cunny" Ben said.

"Thank you Ben. Don't forget to signal the headquarters to make necessary arrangements for our arrest. A green light signal from me will remind you of the best time. I must go now."

"O.K Goodbye and good luck."

Mr. Cunny came out with a bulging bag. He met Mr. Kingsbay drunkenly conversing with the female CID. Within that short period, she was tactfully able to gather all about the business transaction Kingsbay had with Mr. Cunny.

"Sorry to disturb you Mr. Kingsbay" Cunny said as he emerged from the inner room. "If you don't mind, could we go now?"

"Oh! There is no cause for alarm. Lets go please." Kingsbay jumped out like a cat. His attention was more attracted to the bulging bag of money in Cunny's hand. They rushed into the car and it took them just less than 15 minutes to central hotel. After sitting and settling down properly, Mr. Cunny said,

"Lets be serious Mr. Kingsbay. I am going to give you the money, but no double-crossing please. Are you sure the consignments will come in tomorrow?"

"I am very sure. Why should I deceive you? In fact, this is a deal in which witnesses are not necessary, but I don't mind if you call thousands."

"Alright I trust you Mr. Kingsbay. Do you have the receipt here with you?"

"Yes, I do. Its just at the back of my ear. Let me get it please". Mr. Kingsbay dashed out to the car and came back in no time. However it was enough time for Mr. Cunny to send red signals to the headquarters. The signal was to draw the head-quarter's attention for the need to send somebody to tail them. Mr. Kingsbay came back, just in time to catch a point on Mr. Cunny's watch glowing blue. This was actually a reply signal from the headquarters, informing Mr, Cunny that someone was already in the hotel. The man was keeping track of all their activities.

To trace his colleague, Mr. Cunny tactifully raised his head up and looked round. He was pretenciously trying to check with suspiscious looks whether someone was making moves to catch their conversations. He sited the Tail amongst the other hotel customers who were drinking and charting freely. He wore a simple cap which was special in that it bore a small 2mm long camera. The camera was embedded on it, set to record every bit of their transactions. It was directed towards Mr. Cunny and his target with a yellow light emitting from it. Kingsbay observed that Cunny was not at ease and that his attention was drawn away.

"You don't seem to be at ease in pursuing this business Cunny Java"

"I am sorry please" Mr. Cunny pleaded and started paying attention to him again. "You know it could be dangerous if some government watch dogs happen to get into our transaction. I was just trying to see that no one catches our conversation and get to know what we are about to do"

"Ha! Ha! Ha!" Kingsbay laughed teasingly. "you are really a novice in the game. If you don't relax and be at the forefront, you may soon be kicking the ball back into your goal post. To hell with government watch dogs."

Mr. Cunny internally saw Kingsbay as the most foolish target he ever came across.

"Alright, how do I pay you? Definitely not here in the hotel".

"You are right. It was foolish of us to have left your house to end the deal here in the hotel. I agree with you. Apart from government watchdogs, which I doubt if there is any here, there are also some self employed watch gunners." "These people have no time for business transactions. Force is the way to gain their daily bread. The hotel is usually a den for them. How can we count such a huge amount here without falling into their trap?"

"What do you suggest Kingsbay? Let us be quick in our decision. The more I stay here with this bulging bag, the more I risk running into either the watchdogs or watch gunners as you said."

"I suggest that we drive out and complete the rest in the car somewhere".

"That's a good idea, but do you have a touch light?"

"We could use the car light. How do you see it?"

"Perfectly alright, I am tired of carrying this load".

They rose up to go, but before they got to the car, the Tail noticed their movement and followed them.

They drove off, not noticing when he climbed up one tall tree near the hotel. Using the small powerful telecamera, he focused on their tract up to where they stopped. Mr. Cunny knew that his colleague was also good at his work. He therefore made no move to allow Kingsbay suspect anything fishy.

When they stopped at last, Mr. Kingsbay removed the receipt booklet. He quickly wrote a receipt of the sum of one hundred and fifty thousand Naira. Mr. Cunny received the receipt and in return handed him seventy-five brand new bundles of two thousand Naira each. The money was all in twenty Naira notes.

"I have fulfilled mine. Yours tomorrow isn't it?"

"Yes, mine tomorrow and please be rest assured"

"I will provide the labourers but you'll pay their fee for loading and offloading Mr. Kingsbay".

"That's O.K. it makes things easier for me".

"Where do we meet?"

"Along the narrow road leading to Kimba village and under the big Iroko tree"

"I understand. I will be there with an empty lorry for the transfer of the drugs".

"That's alright, be sure to come with the labourers. Ten of them will be alright"

"I won't forget, please take me to the hotel to pick my

bicycle."

"Before we go, allow me to ask just one question please"

"Go ahead" Mr. Cunny said.

"I am surprised you have such money, but you go about riding that old grand father's bicycle. You may also wish to tell me why you appear in begger's cloth." Kingsbay enquired.

"Your observation is good Mr. Kingsbay. I don't want people to know that I am rich. They will kill me for it. Before my father died, he warned me never to let the world see my riches. He said that I could display my wealth only after having three male children."

"How many of them do you have now?"

"I am yet to see any"

"I wish you luck"

"Thank you"

# CHAPTER NINE

# THE DRUG DELIVERY DEAL

AFTER DROPPING MR. CUNNY AT THE CENTRAL HOTEL, Kingsbay drove straight to the hospital drivers' house. That was the driver who usually brings the drug supplies from the headquarters. He was the only person in the whole hospital who had connections with Kingsbay in the drug business. He was almost sleeping off when he heard a knock at the door. As usual, he was expecting Kingsbay that night. Kingsbay knew the day he would arrive with the drugs. The delivery at the hospital was yet to be done the next day.

The driver opened the door and greeted as soon as he saw Kingsbay.

"You are welcomed sir"

"You are also welcomed, Ali.

"How was the road?"

"I had a safe journey, sir"

"Were you successful?"

"Quiet successful sir"

"Hope no one has noticed your arrival yet."

"Not even a fly sir. I have just arrived and the lorry load is still packed at the usual place for security."

"That is very good. I have news for you. A very sweet one indeed"

"What news sir?" Ali asked curiously.

"Before I speak, here is your own share" Kingsbay handed him seven and half bundles of two thousand Naira each in brand new twenty Naira notes. Ali amazingly looked at the huge amount of money. He couldn't comprehend exactly what Kingsbay meant by his share?

"What exactly do you mean by my own share sir?" he asked. They have never made such a large sum of money at once. Could that really be his own or he is dreaming?

"We have a new customer. He has offered the sum of one hundred and fifthy thousand Naira for the whole consignment."Kingsbay lied by not telling the driver that the amount was just an advance. "You now understand why fifteen thousand Naira is yours as the ten percent deal in our agreement."

"You are too good and wonderful. I don't know how to express my thanks to you. However, sir, don't you think giving out the whole consignment is dangerous?"

"No, not at all. I still have some left over from last month's supply. You know it was just three quarters that we put into our business last month. I will issue the left over out, to reflect the in coming consignment. Nobody will suspect anything fishing. Relax Ali, no knife will be drawn to your neck."

"O.K. what is the nature of the deal this time?"

"What do you mean Ali?"

"I mean the part I will play. How shall I deliver the goods?"

"Good, you will drive off to the bush very early tomorrow morning. Take to the narrow road leading to Kimbu village. Stop under the big iroko tree near the road. A private lorry will follow you with about ten labourers. The drugs will be transferred to the private van. That ends your part and I will do the rest."

"After emptying my lorry, I will drive the official vehicle to the store. I hope you will be there to receive the transfer issue voucher (T.I.V) from the headquarters, isn't it?"

"Perfectly right, but don't come to me early. I won't be there earlier than 2.00PM."

"That's enough time for me to reduce my wealth, eating, drinking and relaxing at home before then" he said.

"No problem, but no one should know you are already back from the headquarters."

"Haba, Sir, am I still new to this business? Have full confidence in me please".

"I trust you, Ali. All will be well".

"I also hope so sir. The only slight fear is how to escape completely, now that the whole consignment is envolved"

"I say you should relax Ali. The way out is very simple. As usual I will collect the transfer issue voucher (T.I.V) from you; enter it into the store receipt voucher (SRV), make the necessary entries into the store ledgers and finally issue out the same quantities to the compound nurse. The issue will be distributed in acceptable quantities at various intervals to cover the whole month, just in black and white."

"Lets hope no auditor comes within the month to check"

"No problem Ali, if anyone comes for checking, I will settle him or her. You know me don't you? To be rich is one of the advantages"

"I know you very well, sir. That ends the story" the driver concluded and both of them burst into a big laughter.

Unfortunately for them, they were not aware that Mr. Cunny had tactfully attached another small sef-operating tape recorder to the side mirror of Mr. Kingsbay's car. The recorder sticked into position like a speck of clay and it is detachable only by a special magnetic system.

"I have to go now Ali"

"What says your time sir?"

"Its now 9.15pm."

"You said I don't need to know where the consignment goes finally, isn't it?"

"Yes, not yours, but my business. You must be very tired and I don't want to bother you much. Goodnight"

"Goodnight sir, till tomorrow"

The hospital driver couldn't have a nice sleep that night. When he left Kingsbay, he went straight to Mama Peace's beer parlour. He took two bottles of Gulder and a plate of hot chicken pepper soup. He then proceeded back to his house.

He hurriedly took the pounded yam and the egusi soup his wife offered him and went to bed. He wanted to sleep but he ended up spending half of the night being awake.

He was somehow disturbed about the high risk he was embarking upon with Kingsbay. If the game backfires, will he be able to withstand the repercussion? Kingsbay may be able to absorb the shock, but who is he to face the wrath of conspiracy and theft which will not only lead to his dismissal from work but a very long jail term with no option of fine. Who will take care of his five young children and his wife who was critically sick,

Mallam Ali was tempted to change his mind on the dangerous game Kingsbay was dragging him into. He however, remembered the huge sum of money in his possession and felt otherwise; After all it is worth taking the risk.

Very early in the morning, the driver bravely went and collected the lorry load of drugs. He drove towards the appointed direction with the full hope that Kingsbay was to follow him soon.

Kingsbay was keenly watching the road from the verandah of his house when the lorry passed. He was already dressed up and set for business. He jumped into his old beetle car and drove after the lorry driver who has never failed him.

On the other hand, Mr. Cunny had arranged for ten good CID men who dressed in tattered clothes to pose as the labourers for the loading and off loading of the drugs. A very big CID van was used to convey the labourers and to be used for the collection of the drugs from the hospital lorry. The driver of the van and the ten labourers were waiting at a very strategic place to catch the passing of the hospital lorry and Mr. Kingsbay to the appointed place.

As soon as they noticed their expected targets, they hurriedly rushed into the van which soon drove off after Kingsbays car.

The three vehicles stopped under the Iroko tree. The ten labourers jumped out of the private lorry like hungry cats after a rat. Kingsbay saw how smart the labourers jumped out of the van. They all had a very broad chest with bushy hair. Some of them were fat with hunch backs and flat hairs typical of those who were used for loading and off loading heavy containers.

They all went towards Kingsbay, bowed and respectfully greeted him with all sense of humility. The team leader stepped forward and introduced the team as the labourers sent by Mr. Cunny to transfer the drugs. They bargained and settled for three thousand Naira for the transfer of the drugs from the hospital lorry into the CID van.

The labourers swept into action and before long the job was done. Mr. Kingsbay was very impressed about their performance. They were however left with flat hair and wrinkled faces which were formed as a result of the pressure on them caused by the heavy cartons of drugs. They were all sweating profusely.

"Oga, now na your talk ooh. Our own don finish." The leader of the labourers said. Without any delay, Kingsbay paid them the agreed sum of three thousand Naira. He requested them to follow him for the off-loading as well.

The labourers were specially arranged by Mr. Cunny. All of them were CID members with the Tail of the previous night as the team leader. Their bushy hairs were special wigs hard to identify. The loaded lorry was driven straight to the CID bungalow. They were shown an empty room by the female CID member. She kept Kingsbay company while the drugs were being offloaded. He was wondering why Mr. Cunny was not at home to receive him.

"Where is your master please"

"He went out, but will soon come back. He was expecting you. He told me that you would be here around this time of the day."

"I wish he delays a bit longer, so that we can talk more. By the way, where is your mistress?"

"She has gone overseas for a special course in medicine." She lied because Mr. Cunny was yet to get married."

"Sure, I quite understand. Your master is wise and serious. He is making a good plan for her to come and handle his medicine store."

"There comes my master" She said, pointing to a car coming towards them. "Let's keep apart please. He caught us yesternight and I don't want history to repeat itself."

"Alright, as you wish, but allow me to say I love you. You are naturally built like an angel." He flattered her.

"Thank you sir," she appreciated and flew into the kitchen before Mr. Cunny arrived."

"I am sorry for the delay" Mr.Cunny apologized. "Hope I have not wasted much of your time."

"No,not at all. The drugs are just being off-loaded now. Its not a joke loading and off loading such a large quantity of drugs"

"How are the labourers?"

"Very good. Where did you pick such nice labourers.All working very hard and carefully in handling the cartons of drug. Just hear how they are humming a song and working diligently. We had no damage while loading and same may be the case with offloading."

"Do you usually incur great damages in the hospital when off loading?"

"The hospital labourers usually damage over 30-40% of the monthly consignment while offloading."

"Terrible,why do they do that?"

"Only God knows. Let's go to the offloading room to observe the progress of the work so far."

"Welcome Oga" the team leader said to Kingsbay as they entered." "This na de last Carton" he smiled at Kingsbay while ignoring Mr. Cunny completely."

"No one broke?" Kingsbay asked.

"Even carton sef no scrass Sir" The team leader proudly replied. "The people fearGod do the job".

"You are right and may God bless you all". Kingsbay replied with a smile of joy.

"Thank you sir, but na your turn to play de ball. Time de go and we wan go put hand for belleh sir." The leader complained while rubbing his stomach with his right hand indicating sign of hunger.

"Sure and here you are" Mr. Kingsbay handed to him the sum of four thousand naira instead of the bargained three thousand naira. "You have the extra amount as bonus for good, honest and careful job."

"Thank you sir" all the labourers echoed and ran off at top speed towards a nearby food canteen. Not for food, but just to mark the end of their part. They all knew the notes were marked and were yet to be exchanged for plain currencies in circulation before they can spend them.

Mr. Cunny called Kingsbay into the sitting room and paid him the remaining balance of the deal. Kingsbay bent over the heap of money and was busy counting them in bunches.

"I am still shocked about the amount you said hospital labourers usually break or damage." Mr Cunny remarked to stir up a conversation in the line of damages.

"My brother, 30 to 40% is not a joke." Kingsbay said without looking up. "You can just imagine the number of innocent patients that die as a result of their carelessness" he further lamented. He was immediately interrupted by a strange deep voice.

"And you can imagine the number that die when 100% goes away into your stupid business." Kingsbay and Cunny looked up surprisingly. Their eyes met with those of a fiercely looking policeman. He had a short dangerous gun pointed at the criminals. The bundles of Naira notes in Kingsbay's hand were vigorously vibrating as if they were responding to a very strong oscillating wind.

"You have ruined more lives than death itself." The policeman said. "Will you rise and face the music of your conspiracy, you fools?" Both Kingsbay and Cunny were arrested and were taken to the police station. They were later taken to the Timbo criminal area court.

# CHAPTER TEN
## THE JUDGMENT

"YOU ARE BOTH CHARGED for conspiring and duping Timbo General Hospital of a full lorry load of drugs. Are you guilty or not guilty?" The trial judge asked.

"We are not guilty" Mr. Cunny said.

"What do you have to say Mr. Bay" repeated the judge.

"We are not guilty" Kingsbay answered with conspicuously shaking lips.

"Alright, listen to this and be the judge yourselves." At the order of the trial judge, the court registrar replayed all the important and relevant portions of their discussions during the said business transactions. The information's were recorded by Mr. Cunny's secretary, the wristwatch, the small special automatic tape recorder which was attached to Kingsbay's car and the Tail's report.

"Have you heard all? The trial judge asked the two criminals.

"Yes sir" they answered

"Now judges, pass your ruling" the trial judge pointed to the two. It was only after hearing their voices in connection with the criminal deal,that they knew there was no way out. Both of them pleaded guilty with serious apologies. Kingsbay wondered how these people were able to catch all about their transactions, even his discussions with the hospital driver.

Finally as their penalties, both Kingsbay and Cunny were to receive thirty six strokes of a cane each. In addition, Mr,.

Cunny was to forfeit his house (meaning the CID bungalow) and the whole drugs to the government. Mr. Kingsbay was to refund to the government, the whole sum of two hundred and five thousand Naira, loose his personal medicine store to the government, pay an additional fine of fifty-five thousand Niara and finally to be sentenced to ten years imprisonment with hard labour. The driver who was also brought in to face the judgments, was to pay a fine of twenty thousand Naira and also sentenced to ten years imprisonment.

Mr. Cunny however, pretended to be feeling the penalty of loosing his house and the whole quantity of the drugs he bought.

Mr. Kingsbay hated corporal punishment. He started fainting, more in fear of the strokes of cane than the other penalties. He was to be the first to go and meet the torture master for the strokes. He fearfully imagined how the thirty six strokes were going to land on his buttocks. He even visualized his skin peeling off, blood oozing out as the strokes landed. Just as he was being dragged into the torture room, he heard an unbelievable request by Mr. Cunny.

Mr. Cunny volunteered to receive all the seventy-two strokes on behalf of Mr. Kingsbay and himself.

"Does he mean it?" Kingsbay exclaimed. He felt the security man relaxing his grip. He was no longer being dragged to the torture master. "Could it be true that he was not going to receive the severe corporal punishment?" Kingsbay tried to think of what actually prompted Mr. Cunny to take such a step. He tried to connect it to the introductory part of their conversation at the hotel. But could that be enough reason to offer such a great painful sacrifice? Mr. Cunny's brother for sure was not the only patient attended to. All along Kingsbay had doubted Mr. Cunny as a true friend. His offer to bear such a great pain for him, cleared all doubts in Kingsbay mind. He trusted Mr. Cunny more than ever and graded him as the best of all friends in the world. This marked the beginning of their tight friendship.

Mr. Cunny finally went into the torture room. Instead of receiving the corporal punishment, he met face to face with his CID boss. He offered Mr. Cunny a very warm handshake, congratulating him for a job well done. The boss immediately handed to him a letter of double promotion as a token appreciation from the government.

All the CID officers who participated in that investigation of the drug scandal in Timbo Hospital were adequately rewarded.

Mr. Kingsbay was straight away escorted to the prison yard together with the hospital driver under tight security. Kingsbay was lucky that his ten years jail term only lasted for two and half years. His saviour was the visit of her royal highness the queen of Santial. She visited Timbo Central prison just two and half years during Kingsbay's jail term. Mr. Kingsbay and three others were granted amnesty by her. They were set free.

When Kingsbay came out of prison, he immediately traced Mr. Cunny who took him to his real rented house. He thought Mr. Cunny had actually lost his former beautiful bungalow which was ceased by the government.

"Where is your wife and that your beautiful house girl?" Kingsbay asked.

"It's a pity I lost both of them as a result of the poverty that both of us were thrown into" Mr. Cunny replied.

"Poverty indeed. And yet you even offered to bear thirty six extra strokes on my behalf. I really don't know how to express my thanks to you."

"That is by-gone, Kingsbay lets be more careful in the future" Kingsbay would have been dismissed by the ministry of health but the ministry considered his remorseful apology, his large family, the great hardship he underwent in prison and the fact that he has been a hard working staff. The ministry only suspended him for long with half pay after which he was re -absorbed fully.

Mr. Cunny later married one Miss Adini a few years after Kingsbay was released from the prison. Kingsbay even acted as the best friend during the wedding. He also assisted greatly in lobbying for her employment as ward attendant in Timbo Hospital. Mr. Cunny never knew that Kingsbay had a hidden interest for Adini until time revealed it on the day when Fibina was involved in the blood issue. Thanks to Christopher's wife. Her sickness led to the discovery of Kingsbay's treacherous colour.

# CHAPTER ELEVEN

# CHRISTOPHER'S WIFE NEEDS MEDICAL ATTENTION

CHRISTOPHER WAS A GOOD JOURNALIST. He never missed any interesting scene that comes his way. He never separated with his small special camera which was always loaded with films ready for any emergency.

His newly married wife was in a state of pregnancy. Her pregnancy had reached an advanced stage. Her expected day of delivery (EDD) was still about a month ahead. Surprisingly she fell into an unexpected labour one night. This was the same night that sister Fibina was battling with the repercussion of wrong blood transfusion in Timbo hospital.

She was bleeding profusely and unable to walk. It was getting very late in the night. There were no more town taxis plying the street. Christopher had no vehicle to convey her to the hospital which was about three kilometers away.

Mr. Christopher was a neighbour to Mr. Cunny the CID officer. He knew Cunny was very generous and kind. He always assisted Christopher greatly when it came to serious cases like that. Mr. Christopher knew Cunny had bought one second new car to replace his old bicycle. Since the car was bought, Mr. Christopher had not asked his neighbour for any favour.

Christopher knew Mr. Cunny would be willing to convey his wife to the hospital,but he only doubted whether Cunny would be at home at such a late hour. He usually went to drop his wife Adini at the hospital and Sometimes he delayed his return home after dropping her. Christopher was aware that Adini was on night duty that faithful day. However, to rule out all doubts, Christopher had to check on his neighbour.

He rushed to Mr. Cunny's house. Luckily for him, Cunny was in because he saw Cunny's car neatly packed near the door. He hopefully knocked at the door,

"Who are you please?" Mr. Cunny asked. He wondered who would be his guest at such late hour of the night. He himself had just returned from the hospital where he dropped his wife for her night duty. He heard the voice of a familiar person.

"Its Christopher your neighbour please"

"Oh come in, smartest man of the press." Mr. Cunny quickly rushed to the door. He happily looked into Christopher's face expecting same gesture from him but on the contrary he saw fear written all over his usually jovial neighbour.

"What is the problem please?" Cunny asked greatly surprised. He was afraid his neighbour was really in trouble in one way or the other. Christopher wore a very pale face with almost dry cracking lips. He looked very worried. Christopher, a tall medium size man, usually jovial. Sweet smiles usually radiate from his lips whenever one meets him. These were some of the qualities that made people like him. They say, these qualities were also contributory factors to his great success in journalism. Mr. Cunny was one of his many admirers. He was wonderful when he put a scene into writing. Their daily papers were always being scrambled for. Every one would like to read what Christopher wrote for the day. He made a lot of money for the press company to which he belonged, especially when any of his write-ups were put in the front page.

"Good evening Mr. Cunny" Christopher said. "I am really very sorry to disturb you at such a late hour of the night."

"Good evening Chris. I was shocked by the way you ap-

peared, that I couldn't greet you in the first place. You don't
need to mention at all, you are highly welcomed. Please
sit down and may I still asked why you looked that much
worried?"

"It's my wife."

"What Happened?"

"She had just been stricken by a serious sickness. She complained of abdominal pain and backache. Worst of all, she has
started bleeding very profusely indicating that the baby was
in danger"

"Her EDD perhaps"

"Not yet. Still about a month to go."

"I highly sympathize with you Chris. She requires hospital
attention, isn't it?"

"Very quick indeed and my problem is transportation"

"I know Chris. Thank God that my car which was usually troublesome, is in good condition today. In fact, I was just
back with it from Timbo hospital where I dropped my wife for
her night duty. She will be there to assist your wife."

"I will also take along my mother and one small boy to
keep her company at the hospital please."

"No problem Chris. The car is roomy enough. Go and get
them prepared, I will be there in a minute."

Christopher thanked Cunny very much and rushed back
home. Mr. Cunny quickly removed his night gown, dressed
up nicely and in less than ten minutes he was at Christopher's
house. He collected his neighbour and the family. It took him
less than five minutes to arrive Timbo hospital.

Instead of the maternity ward, the sick woman was taken to
the female medical ward. Mr. Cunny took them there so that
his wife Adini could give a helping hand. They entered the
ward when the two nursing sisters were still on the handing

over process. They were still waiting for the compound nurse to take the final decision on forcing the drawer open.

The compound nurse being awaited for was Kingsbay. After his release from the prison, Kingsbay was not completely dismissed from service. He lost amongst other things his acting duty as the hospital pharmacist. It was only after a long time that he assumed work as a compound nurse again.

CHAPTER TWELVE

# THE DOCTOR ENGAGED?

AFTER A CLOSE EXAMINATION OF THE POOR SICK WOMAN, sister Sentoria knew it was more of a maternity case than medical. However, she decided to send for the doctor to examine her before any re-arrangement could be done. She sent one of the night security men in place of the ward attendants, to call the doctor. The two attendants had earlier been sent to call the compound nurse. They were yet to come back.

"Which doctor should I call sister?" asked the security man

"Doctor Mali please. Check for him in his consulting room first. If you don't see him there, you should proceed to his house. Please be fast." The security man rushed off and soon returned with a complain.

"It appears the doctor is seriously at work. I heard a moaning voice of a woman. I knocked several times, without an answer from within."

"What! this woman's case is serious and very critical and yet the doctor seems to be very busy with another one" sister Sentoria said in surprise.

"But why couldn't he answer to say that he was busy?" Fibina asked.

"That's what puzzled, me too, sister" Sentoria replied. Christopher and his friend Cunny became worried. The mother in-law was busy battling with the restless condition of her daughter in-law.

"Since the ward attendants have delayed in the compound

office, why don't you check on the doctor yourself" sister Fibina suggested to sentoria.

"That's Just exactly what I had in mind. I have to go and check on him personally." Sister Sentoria called upon the security man to go with her. Mr.Christopher decided to follow them too. Mr. Cunny, sister Fibina and Christopher's mother were left to look after the sick woman. When Sentoria and the other two got to the doctor's room, they also heard the reported voice of a woman. Sentoria decided to open the door without excuse. They saw the unexpected scene.

Doctor Mali jumped down from the examination bed, exposing the almost naked full length of Kimba's body. She was lying helplessly on the bed gazing at the spectators. The doctor didn't know where to hide his face. His body was shaking like one suddenly struck by a high fever. Kimba felt like fussing into the wooden examination bed. She wished she were just a mere log of wood. Dr. Mali and Kimba were both blinded with unbearable shame.

Christopher forgot all, except the scene in front of them. He swung into action despite his pending sorrows. The flash light of his camera was decorating the room as it went on and off several times.

Doctor Mali was thrown into a mystery with un-coordinated thoughts. He was confused. He looked very stupid in the midst of the spectators. However, he was able to recall to memory, some of the PMO's stern warnings. One of those that came to his mind was in connection with staff flirtations.

Unfounded rumours were circulating in town, that Timbo hospital was highly polluted with cases of flirtations. It became the talk of the town. It was said that the flirting was not only within the staff alone but also between the staff and patients' relatives.

When the rumour was first reported to the P.M.O, he dismissed it as baseless. It was only when he heard it for the second time that he took action. He decided to issue a stern warning for the benefit of doubt. He summoned all the senior staff to a meeting. He seriously warned them against any attempt to tarnish the good image of Timbo hospital. He emphasized much about the flirtation rumours circulating all over the town. Unfortunately, Dr. Mali was the first to suggest dismissal penalty to any defaulter and that was agreed upon. The P.M.O urged all the senior staff to be very vigilant. They were to report any suspicious moves as soon as they observed them.

One night, despite the warnings, one female ward attendant was caught red handed. She was caught with one fairly old security man. Both of them were dismissed out-right.

The case was later reported to the headquarters. The report gave details of; the earlier rumours; the P.M.O's warnings; the violation of the warnings by the two junior staff caught red handed; the outright action of the hospital authority on them and a request for directives to be carried out in cases of senior staff involvement.

A letter was soon received from the headquarters as a reply to the report. Consequently, the hospital authority quickly summoned all the staff, including all junior and senior staff to another crucial meeting. The following directives from the headquarters were read to them.

(i). Any junior staff found messing up in the hospital, even if it was a mere exchange of love words, be dismissed forth with by their immediate senior officers.

(ii). Any senior staff similarly found wanting, should be suspended immediately by the hospital authority pending the decision of the headquarters.

(iii). Any NYSC member falling into the said act of indiscipline, will have his term of service extended by three years. He/she will have no employment opportunities in any part of the state.

Immediately after the above directives and warnings were read to the staff, Timbo hospital was transformed into one of the best health institutions in the state. For a long time, there were no more detrimental rumours about the hospital. However, Dr. Mali and Kimba turned the revamped good name of the hospital back to bad, just over night. Kimba thought of Adini and the compound nurse. They left her at the doctor's room and proceeded to the female medical ward.. "If Adini really went straight to the ward, it puzzles me why sister Sentoria should come for the doctor by herself, instead of sending her" Kimba contemplated doubtfully in her mess.

# CHAPTER THIRTEEN

## CHRISTOPHER'S FIRST SON

MR. CUNNY WHO WAS LEFT LOOKING after Christopher's wife became un-easy. He hasn't seen his wife since they arrived. He knew she works in the female medical ward. That was the ward they were waiting for the doctor. He decided to inquire from sister Fibina. He met her sitting by the staff table full of thoughts. She was wearing a very dull sickly look.

"Excuse me sister" he said.

"You look sick, is anything the matter?"

"No, not at all. I am just tired. I have been working since afternoon and I want to hand over and go home now"

"You are being delayed?"

"Yes we are still waiting for the compound nurse to come"

"I see, but sister, may I know where Mrs. Adini Cunny has gone to, please?"

"She was sent out with one ward attendant to call the compound nurse"

"How long ago sister?"

"That was some thirty minutes ago, it puzzles me, they are not yet back."

Mr. Cunny believed that his wife would be in a better position to care for their neighbour's wife. He knew they were very tight friends.

"My wife will shade tears if she knew about her friend's critical condition" he thought. He had to find her by all means.

"If you don't mind sister, may I ask your favour to lead me to the compound nurse office?" Cunny pleaded. "You know this sick woman is my neighbour's wife and she is a good friend to my wife, just as I am to her husband. I am sure my wife Adini doesn't know that her friend is here very sick. Please help me to fetch her."

"I am at your service and you at mine." Fibina replied with an obviously dull smile. "I was looking for someone to escort me there. Come, let's go please".

Mr. Cunny left the sick woman with Christopher's mother and the small boy who came along with them from home.

"Excuse me mum" he said. "I am going out and I will soon be back." Cunny told his neighbour's mother.

"Where are you going my son?" The old mother asked. "Your friend is out and you also want to leave. Am I left with this load lone?"

"Don't worry mum. I want to fetch my wife who works in this ward. She could be of better help to us please." Mr Cunny said and left with sister Fibina for the compound office.

Surprisingly, just immediately they left, Christopher's wife fell into true labour. Both sister Sentoria and sister Fibina were away. There was no more trained staff around to receive the delivery. The old woman didn't know where to send for them. Who can she even send? She looked round and saw no one who could help. Apart from the small boy who accompanied them from home, the whole ward was filled with patient s lying helplessly on their sick beds. All the patient relatives like Sofa and Abu were deep asleep near their sick relatives. The old mother couldn't distinguish the sick from their relatives. She however, sent the boy out and tried her traditional method of conducting delivery. The woman soon gave birth safely to a big baby boy.

After exhaustively covering the wonderful scene in Dr. Mali's room with his efficient camera, Christopher suddenly remembered his sick wife. He rushed back to the female medical ward where she was. When he came near the said ward, he heard a cry of the newborn baby. He immediately developed an imagination that he was going to the wrong ward.

"This could be the children ward or the maternity". He thought. I must have lost my way. Surely it will be very embarrassing to get into any of these wards without anyone specific to see. Christopher ran back to the confused Dr. Mali's room to get help. He saw that a few more crowds had gathered there to witness what had happened. Christopher spared some seconds to take a few more snap shots. He requested the security man to escort him to the right ward. He actually confessed that he couldn't trace the female medical ward alone. The man led him through the same path leading to the ward that he was afraid to enter. Christopher had to ask him.

"Are you sure we are going to the ward where my wife lies sick?"

"Yes sir"

"Not the children or the maternity ward?" Christopher asked doubtfully.

"What makes you think we are going to those wards and not the female medical ward sir?"

"Because I heard the cry of a new born baby from the ward you are leading me to"

"Trust and believe me sir. I have been in this hospital for twenty years. How can I mistake one ward for another?" the security man replied confidently. Just then the baby cried to their hearing."

"Do you hear that?" Chris suddenly asked. "How can I believe you that we are not approaching maternity?"

"We are not sir"

"Look man, I want to see my wife quickly without un-necessary delays."

"Cheer up sir we are really going to the female medical ward where your wife was left"

"Well, let me keep by you", Christopher said.

"You know she came in with a heavy stomach. My guest is that it could be your child" the security man predicted.

"Keep aside jokes please. She told me that her EDD is still a month to go. Her sickness, I know is a sign of danger for the baby. Instead of pitying the condition, you are here cracking impossible jokes" Mr. Christopher said with a slightly angry tune.

"I was only wishing you a good omen, but I am sorry if it hurts you sir" the security man regretted what he said.

"I accept your wishes but I feel it's too early to talk of that."

"The sure thing is that your wife's case has more to do with maternity than medical ward. Here we are. Let's go in to see what's going on." They entered the ward.

Mr. Christopher' couldn't believe his eyes. He saw his mother holding a baby. His mother welcomed him with a happy smile.

"My daughter has given me another son." She said to him. "Sit down my dear son and admire your first baby boy."

Christopher couldn't speak for some time. At last he looked at the security man and said to his mother; "Mummi, this man is a prophet. He predicted this before we came in." Christopher was covered all over with overwhelming joy. His lips were radiating smiles of gratitude to God.

The security man was also smiling, but more to the pride of his fulfilled prediction. He was imagining himself as a prophet indeed.

Christopher bent down to get hold of the baby, but he was quickly cautioned by his mother not to do so yet.

"Don't touch him yet my son," she said quickly. "He needs to the bathed for the second time before any male touch, please."

"You are the greatest doctor Mum" Christopher said excitedly. "May God bless you and extend your life on earth."

"Thank you dear, but where did you go?"

"We went to fetch the doctor Mum."

"And you delayed that much without finding him?"

"We saw him Mummy, but the reason for our delay is very funny. I will tell you about it when we get home. The story may even appear in tomorrow's papers. By the way where is my neighbour Mr. Cunny?"

"He said he was going to the compound office to fetch his wife."

"Did he go before or after the baby's arrival Mummy?"

"Your son came just immediately after his departure."

"Mummy, I can't wait here until he comes. I know the compound office. I must get there straight away to give him this good news."

"I understand my son. It's no joke becoming a father for the first time. Be careful how you walk, some excitements are dangerous my son.I will not be surprised if you find yourself falling on the corridor.

"I can see your point mother. I will be extra careful he said and off he went."

# CHAPTER FOURTEEN

## AT THE COMPOUND OFFICE

CHRISTOPHER MOVED VERY FAST TOWARD THE COMPOUND OFFICE. He surprisingly caught up with Mr. Cunny and sister Fibina before they got to the compound office. They were shocked to see Christopher running after them. Immediately Cunny saw the haste with which his neighbour was running towards them, he suspected danger. They waited to hear him.

"Could it be that his sick wife has brought them bereavement?" Cunny thought. He quickly looked at his neighbour and saw a sign which told a different story. Christopher approached them with sweet smiles, radiating joy and not sorrow. Cunny became releaved. He shook his friend happily as their hands met.

"What's the news?" he whispered to his friend.

"Both good and bad" Christopher replied.

A current of fear flew through Cunny again.

"Tell me the good one first." Cunny was anxious to hear.

"Of course, I couldn't have started with the bad one which doesn't concern me but it is also for my benefit, the good one is part of me and shall continue to remind me of the happiest day in my life."

"Please tell me Chris."

"Don't call me Christopher any longer, but the father of ….."

"You mean your wife has put to birth?"

"Exactly, and a bouncing baby boy for that matter."

"Congratulations the father of:........." Cunny called Christopher the way he wanted to be called. It was so funny that they all burst into laughter. Sister Fibina who was following their jokes, also joined them laughing despite her burden.

"I am told you were going to fetch your wife."

"Yes, let's go on to call her to join in the jubilation,"

"Before we go on, may we know how you convinced the doctor to come to your aid please". Sister Fibina asked.

"Which doctor sister?"

"The one you followed sister Sentoria to call."

"He didn't come at all."

"Fibina and Cunny held their lips with immense amazement."

"What made him so occupied in his consulting room or you didn't see him at all?" Cunny asked

"That is the subject of the other side of the coin"

"The bad part of the news isn't it?" Fibima came in.

"Yes it was a funny, but piteous scene." Christopher said.

"What really happened please? You know we are anxious"

"It's a long story, but in short, we caught him with one female ward attendant in a shameful act."

"Really" his two audience echoed with wide open eyes. They bewailed the story.

"Do you know the ward attendant involved?" Fibina ask to know more.

"I don't know her, but she was called by the name Kimba or so"

"Kimba!" Fibina exclaimed. "It puzzles me. How did she get to the doctor's consulting room?"

"You know her properly then? Christopher said."

Yes she is one of the attendants working in the same ward with me."

"Where was she supposed to be?

Cunny asked with fear. He was wondering whether that could be the attendant who was sent out together with his wife to call the compound nurse.

"She is the attendant we sent out with your wife Adini to call the compound nurse. How could they have gone to the doctor's room instead?"

"Did you see my wife at that cinema, Chris?"

"No, I didn't see her. It may be she left your wife waiting for her at the compound office" Christopher replied.

"Let's hope so." Cunny said with a suspicious tone.

"So it was sister Sentoria who received the delivery of your new baby?"

"No,none of the medical personnel in this hospital took part in bringing the apple of my eye into the world."

"You mean you personally assisted your sick wife alone?" Fibina asked.

"No, not me, I got to the ward when the child was already breathing the world's atmospheric air."

"Who took the delivery then?" Fibina was curious to get the details. She knew that woman was too sick to deliver without aid. She also underrated the capabilities of Christopher's old mother. She graded her as too old and too primitive to carry out such a job that needs expertise with years of good training and experience.

"My old mother, the greatest original doctor in the world."

"Your mother!" Fibina was bewildered.

"Yes, that old, but brainy woman did it single handedly"

"I owe that woman a special gift" Mr. Cunny said. Let us now go to fetch my wife please.

They rushed to the compound office at last. Sister Fibina knocked at the door and swiftly opened it. The team of three went in and were shock at what their eyes fell on.

A similar scene as was at Dr. Mali's room.Adini had already put on her pant. She was just about to put her under wear when they were caught unaware. Her blue uniform gown and the white apron were still lying on the floor. She stood still, holding her brassier in one hand and her underwear on the other hand. She was in a complete state of obscurity. She didn't know exactly what to do next. Her limbs were vibrating as if they had no bones. She caused her eyes for sighting her husband amongst the spectators. As soon as her eyes fell on him her body stiffened. She stood as a planted carved log of wood; speechless and with her mouth as dry as a chest nut. Her lips started cracking with unbearable fear. "Oh God!" she thought deep in her mind. "My work is at stake as well as my matrimonial home."

On the other hand, the team met Kingsbay the compound nurse struggling to put on his white pair of uniform trousers. One of his legs was already inside and the other one still outside the trouser. He was standing with his head bent to the knees exposing his almost naked buttocks, bearing a blood red pant.

As soon as the spectators came in, Kingsbay shockingly staggered backwards. The other leg also came out of the trousers and he didn't know when he released the trousers to the ground. He was thrown into a perplexed condition, he appeared blinded with confused thoughts. With vigorously shaking hands he bent down trying to trace the fallen trouser. His legs seem to have been planted in one place. He couldn't move them, but was blindly stretching his arms all around looking for it. At last, he found it, but his shaking hands became too weak to lift it up. Trying hard to trace the upper edge of the clothe, Kingsbay only succeeded in dragging it here and there on the floor. To the spectators, it appears he succeeded in only dusting the floor with his pair of trousers. They compared him to a house wife cleaning or mopping the floor with a rag.

Kingsbay dared not lift up his face again to meet the three people who had just come in. He recognized two of them at first sight. Those were sister Fibina and Mr. Cunny the so-called best friend of his. He wouldn't be surprised, if Mr. Cunny whose wife he took, decided to pierce a sharp knife through his heart. "Yes I deserve such a fatal action," he thought. "I don't expect her husband to play the part of the almighty God to forgive such a grave offence." Mr.Kingsbay felt as if he was enclosed into one dark room, surrounded by very thick walls and with no doors and windows for ventilation. He felt himself suffocating. His confused thoughts wondered to the suffering he had, when he was arrested in connection to the drug scandal. He recollected how Mr. Cunny had offered to bear thirty six extra lashes on his behalf for the sake of their friendship. Here he was, repaying him with treason. What a public disgrace.

"Oh! Surely, there is no way out again. I am gone, I am ruined, I have thrown my work into a deadly trap again", he lamented inwardly.

The three spectators couldn't believe their eyes. They were all shocked. They all lifted their hands to their mouths, held them tight with their eyes wide open in amazement. The only one who didn't view the scene as surprisingly new, was Mr. Christopher the press man. He had watched a similar life display at Dr. Mali's office, just a moment ago. Sister Fibina nodded to show that she then understood the reason why the ward attendants delayed. Her head was continuously swinging back and front.

Mr.Cunny couldn't bear it any longer, seeing his wife involved in such a disgraceful act. He couldn't believe that Kingsbay whom he trusted as his best friend, was such a deceitful beast. He wondered how many times these fools have been together like this. No wonder Mr. Kingsbay had never failed to visit their house. Mr.Kingsbay had advised him to allow Adini to take up a job at Timbo hospital. That crook, in the name of friendship, had told him that Adini could be employed as a ward attendant He had promised to secure the job for her even though there was only one vacancy left and despite her poor qualification. He said many were fighting to get it. He actually succeeded in getting her the job but all for a hidden agenda.

"Oh!God!" Mr. Cunny exclaimed. "I thought he was acting as a good friend to me. I trusted him fully.Little did I know that he was a green snake in a green grass. Little did I know that by securing her a place in the hospital, he was actually dressing a bed for themselves with a devil's Dunlop mattress. I don't think any of them deserves to live." Mr.Cunny concluded and furiously dashed into action.

Angrily he looked at his wife as an injured lion for about five seconds and swiftly, he turned towards Kingsbay with a fearfully clenched fist. His lower lip was tightly held between the two set of teeth. His eyes protruded out as if to get them detached from their sockets. Without further delay, he gave Kingsbay what he had long expected. The anger activated energy of his clenched fist went straight to Kingsbay's face. The nasty blow forced Kingsbay to an upright position briefly. The trouser was immediately released and left on the floor. From the real upright position, Kingsbay finally landed flat on his back. His head crashed unto the hard cement floor leaving him lying as stiff as a dead log. Mr. Cunny turned to his wife and said; "as for you woman, get prepared to meet him in the grave for your second wedding."

The accumulated fears in Adini finally manifested themselves in a funny way. The chains of fear seem to have gathered and transformed themselves into a sort of liquid. They forced their way out inform of urine. The liquid wetted her pant and flow down her thighs. It ended up making a pole on the floor. She knew what was going on, but couldn't move an inch from where she stood. She was stupidly gazing at her spectators and silently awaiting her own share of the husband's reaction.

Sister Fibina tried hard to control herself, but she couldn't help laughing at Adini's funny display.

Mr. Christopher never lost a minute of any scene. His small efficient camera was once more decorating the scene with several flash lights. Christopher, however pitied his neighbour Mr. Cunny whose wife had really brought him great embarrassment. Despite these, the press man was partly glad. The two similar happenings that night in Timbo hospital, will give very good stories for their daily papers. The sales will surely be great.

The spectators silently waited for Kingsbay to recover. After a very long time, Kingsbay opened his eyes, but he couldn't see properly. His eye lids had swollen up, covering his eye balls almost completely. Kingsbay looked like one whose eye lids were suffering from several bee stings.

The principal medical officer had arrived to witness both incidences. He first of all saw Dr.Mali and Kimba before coming to Kingsbay and Adini. After absorbing enough information about all the happenings, he immediately took an interim decision. All the staff involved, were to be detained under strict guidance by the security men pending further actions.

The PMO took over the duty of Dr. Mali and Mr. Kingsbay for the rest of the night. He therefore went with the two nursing sisters to tackle the locked drawer issue.

# CHAPTER FIFTEEN
## THE LOCKED DRAWER

CHRISTOPHER'S WIFE HAD NO COMPLICATION following her safe delivery. She was discharged to go home. As a good press man, Christopher was interested in the locked drawer issue. He was lucky that his friend Mr. Cunny was also interested in the case. Both of them lingered in the hospital for sometime. Christopher didn't know that Cunny was a CID.

The PMO, brought out a bunch of keys from his office. The keys were tried one after the other into the drawer's key hole, but none fitted to open it. Many more keys were brought and tried. Fortunately after a long trails, one of the keys fitted into the key hole and clicked the drawer open.

Sister Fibina was actually not sure whether she was the one who locked the drawer. It could have been locked by someone else. If so, what of if that person decided to leave her an empty drawer? Fibina was very afraid and her body was shaking in response to the fear in her. She was asked to pull out the un-locked drawer. She tried hard to control her shaking hands but in vain. She stretched her hand to pull out the drawer. The attempt to stop her hands from shaking, was betrayed by the drawer itself. Instead of coming out smoothly, it was vibrating noisily to the tune of her shaking fore-limb.

Everybody including the PMO wondered why Fibina was that much afraid. The panic displayed by her, created elements of suspicion in their minds "Could she have been pretending that she locked the money in?" her spectators wondered.

Finally she drew out the drawer which was over shadowed by many curious eyes. All struggling to look into it. Sister Fibina's fear was aggravated as soon as the drawer was out. She was dumbfounded. She dared not look up to face the anxious spectators. She was gazing at the empty drawer with tears of panic. Her right, vibrating hand was un-consciously brushing the bottom of the drawer. She wished the PMO was not there. She hated the presence of the press man whose camera seemed to have un-limited films. She compared her case with that of Adini in the compound office. Adini's was better she drew her mind back to the blood issue. Abu had reported the case to the PMO who had started making enquiries. "And here, I am also to answer for lost government revenue. Over six hundred naira to be accounted for." What a chain of misfortunes. At a time when the bell of retrenchment was seriously calling for defaulters. "Oh poor Fibina"she thought. "Why only you in the whole wide world to be crowned with these thorns of problems?"

Christopher didn't miss any scene. He thanked his camera for enduring the continuous usage without developing any fault. He had never believed in the saying that 'Every disappointment is a blessing' until that night. He swore never to dispute that saying again. Was it not true that his wife's sickness (a disappointment) led to multiple blessings? He smiled as he pictured himself being a father for the first time. He also pictured how his papers were definitely going in for bigger sales. The scenes he gathered that night were many and good enough to attract customers for the next six or more months. The front pages would carry in bold letters such attractive headings as follows;

i. Top officers caught red handed in Timbo hospital.

ii. Two house wives likely to be fired for adultery.

iii. A doctor's consulting room turned into a den for sex.

iv. A working class housewife swims in a pole of urine for panic.

v. A sexy compound nurse mops his office floor.

vi. Timbo hospital polluted with staff flirtations.

vii. Mysterious disappearance of government revenue.

All the spectators were silently observing Fibina's funny reactions to the disappeared government revenue. The PMO was first to break the silence.

"Are you sure you locked the money in that drawer?" He asked Fibina.

"Yes doctor I did. I made sure I removed the keys after locking it." She lied."

"Where did you put the keys then?" The PMO asked again

"I put them into my uniform pocket"

"Then what next?"

"I rushed out to attend to an emergency case and I didn't know the keys fell off. I only discovered the keys were gone after arresting the situation."

"Don't you think you might have rushed off leaving the keys on the drawer?" The PMO continued

"That could be a possibility, doctor"

"Who and who were around when you locked the drawer?"

"Nearly all the evening shift staff of this ward were around but I rushed off to tackle the urgent case with all of them. The only none staff who was also around was a patient's relative. He was peeping through that door while standing near his sister, the patient."

"Do you know his name?"

"No doctor, but I could easily find out from the patient" Fibina quickly said. She was slightly relieved because the

PMO's questions seem to give her some measure of trust.

"Go and find out his name quickly"

Sister Fibina jumped up like a cat, making everyone laugh. She rushed to the patient's bed. What a luck for her, the patient was still awake. After a brief dialogue with the patient, sister Fibina was able to get the name of the said relative.She also gathered that the man had disappeared during the blackout that engulfed the ward some moments ago.The one that occurred during the confusion about the blood case.

"Where do you think he went?" Fibina enquired.

"I don't know, but he stays with his junior brother in town."

"Does he usually go there every night?"

"Yes, he could be there I believe". The patient was answering in good faith, ignorant of why her brother was being sought for. Fibina would have asked more questions but she feared to cause a delayance to the doctor. She rushed back to the centre of attraction. She saw that many more staff were pouring in from the other wards to witness the scene.

"His name is Murvi doctor" she said under a heavy breathe.

"Where is he now?"

"The patient said that he might now be with his junior brother in town, doctor."

# CHAPTER SIXTEEN

## THE WANTED MURVI

MURVI HAD NEVER HANDLED SUCH A LARGE SUM OF MONEY. Immediately he got hold of the money, he proceeded to his junior brother's house. He wanted to leave Timbo town that night or very early the following morning. He lied to his brother that he was going home to fetch more money. The hospital requirements were increasing daily and he had no money to settle them.

"I am going to the hospital to keep our sister company for the night" he said "I might proceed from there for home early tomorrow morning."Murvi was confidently sure that no one saw him removing the government revenue. Therefore nobody will suspect him even if he went back to the hospital.

He packed his properties and actually left for the hospital. Ignorant of the latest developments in the hospital, Murvi felt confident and relaxed, typical of old crooks.

Murvi arrived the hospital just when the PMO was about to send out three security men to fetch him. One of the men knew Murvi very well and even knew where Murvi stays in town.

Immediately Murvi entered the ward, the man who knew him shouted to the others; "here he comes." All eyes were turned to him. He sensed an atmosphere of danger. It suddenly dawned on him that his nefarious action had been discovered. He was probably declared a wanted person and so he didn't wait to see who was shouting and to whom.

He turned swiftly and took to the door. He missed the entrance and crashed his head against the wall near the door. A sudden cracking headache broke through his fore head. He however succeeded in getting through the door, and took to his heels. He didn't go far when he crash-landed again on the floor of the corridor. Before he stood up to run again, the three security men were already on him. In the face of danger, Murvi seemed to have developed a lion's strength.

His first blow, landed on the face of the security man who knew him. It was really a heavy blinding smash. The victim yelled, fell backwards and finally landed with his back on the hard concrete corridor, bruising his head.

"Hush!" the security man exclaimed, "he was not as strong as this before." The other two continued with the fight.

Christopher had followed them, but he had no time to help in the fight. His camera was instead disturbing the fight by blinding their eyes with numerous flashes. He was once more formulating in his mind some good newspaper headlines as follows;

i. Suspect with a lion's might.

ii. Three watch dogs bullied by one spectator.

Before the PMO and the others got to the scene, Murvi had succeeded in overpowering the security men. The fight lasted for seconds only. The three security men were badly injured. They were all left to receive treatment at the male surgical ward.

Murvi ran off at top speed. A noisy crowd was pursuing him. The spectators, including hospital workers and some patients' relatives all went after him. Apart from that security man, now lying sick, none of those pursuing Murvi could recognize him. Sister Fibina who saw him for the first time that night, couldn't recollect his appearance.

Murvi was a very wise thief. As he was running, he kept his ears open to the general comments of his pursuers. He soon discovered that none of them knew who exactly he was. None, not even the PMO and his hospital workers. As he was running, he was also planning for the best means of fusing into the crowd. Since he would not be recognized, he could play safe that way.

He knew that the hospital premises was strongly fenced round. It had only one gate which could have been heavily guided by then. The only alternative for him was to play the trick of joining the crowd.

Murvi looked back and saw that the crowds were still a bit far away from him. He took advantage of a wall-post at a dark corner. He quickly sneaked behind the post and stood as stiff as a log of wood. His hands were placed by the sides downwards as one called to attention. His action was too swift for the approaching crowd to notice.

As soon as those leading the crowd passed by him near the wall post, he quickly slipped into the crowd. Tactifully, he joined in their conversations and utterances about the thief. The little rest he had during his brief stay behind the post, gave him great relief. It enabled him to control his panic stricken lips which could have otherwise betrayed him when speaking.

The crowd got to the gate without finding Murvi. The security gatemen said he didn't get to them. The PMO was furious. He thought Murvi was still within the hospital premises. He instructed the security gatemen not to allow anyone to go out or come in. All the spectators were to be vigilant. They were to get hold of anyone with suspicious movements.

Murvi felt completely trapped. He must think of another way out. He started contemplating on the best method of escape. He could provoke the security men to a fight, to create confusion. This could aid his escape. Before the crowd finally dispersed, Murvi took a brave move to draw their attention. He started challenging the said thief and the security gate men in a provocative manner. "We relatives of patients also fall victims of people with such dubious characters. They rob us of our money and properties," he said. "I suggest that these equally dubious, so-called security gate men be properly interrogated to rule out conspiracy. They should be held responsible if that wanted thief is not found within the hospital premises. They could have intentionally or carelessly allowed the devil to escape and pretentiously fool us that they didn't see him."

The PMO saw some sense in Murvi's prediction, but he thought it was too early to lay blames. He must exhaust all other means of finding the culprit before pointing accusing fingers to possibilities of conspiracy.

Christopher was the only person at the gate who could recognize Murvi. He must have seen him during the fight with the security men, but he was too busy to remember the strange face. The last speaker had a very close resemblance to the wanted culprit, but Christopher was not too sure. He kept mute to be on the safe side.

One of the security gate men felt offended by Murvi's detrimental comments. He displayed a very angry face at Murvi. He felt like eating Murvi alive. Murvi noticed his reaction and was glad that the planned trick was yielding results. He ordered the said security man to go out of the gate and buy for him a stick of cigarette from a nearby provision store. The store was left open that much late because the sales boy fell asleep leaving the door open with the lights on.

The angry security man couldn't control his temper any longer. He started quarrelling, abusing and calling Murvi all sort of names.

That was exactly what the crook wanted. He intentionally wanted to cause commotion, which could aid his escape. He retaliated more harshly than the security man. He shouted and uttered greater provocative abuses to the security men in general. The gatemen also responded in line with Murvi's wishes.

When the exchange of dangerous words were getting to a serious fight, the PMO had to intervene. After bringing the situation under control, the PMO thought the best solution was to allow Murvi buy the cigarette by himself. It never occurred to him that Murvi was the culprit.He ignorantly ordered the gatemen to allow Murvi to go and buy the cigarette by himself.

The crook became very alert. It appears his plan was going to yield an easy good fruit without further rancour. He was thanking his gods in mind, because once he is outside of the gate no Jupiter will catch him. He didn't care who played kindness or cruelty to him. All he cared for was the six hundred naira stocked in his pocket. The security men were not happy and ready to obey the order.

"You have just told us not to allow anyone go out or come in through the gate doctor." They complained. They hated to do a thing that will please their enemy.

"I have given you an order and not just a request. You should allow this man to go and buy the cigarette while I am still here. After he has retuned and I am away there should be no going out or coming in again"

"Please doctor, we are not refusing to open the gate for him but you know that the tricks of crooks are many. Prevention is better than cure. However, if you insist, we don't mind doing as you say." one of the gate men said.

"Who are you calling crook?" Murvi flared up. "Are you trying to retaliate what I said about you corrupt, good for nothing gatemen?" If your conscience is guilty let me say it again that all the culprits involved in tonight's episode, should be brought to book. They should all face the wrath of the law including the fake and dubious security men. Mark you, I am not eager to go outside the gate. That is, if your big but empty head will agree to go and buy the cigarette for me. I am surprised that you are too heady to obey a simple order from a PMO. How are you better than a fool then?" Murvi concluded.

The security men were once more stirred up to fight, but they feared to react in the presence of the PMO. They were all livid.

The PMO observed that history was trying to repeat itself. He gave a stronger order to the security gatemen. Little did he know that he was letting the cat out of the cage.

"Could you open that gate for this man to get what he wants?" The PMO shouted at them with an angry tune. They obeyed reluctantly with out further complain.

# CHAPTER SEVENTEEN

# MURVI OUTSIDE THE GATE

MURVI AMAZINGLY WALKED THROUGH THE GATE. He couldn't believe himself that he was actually outside the gate. "Just alone without anyone following me?" he whispered to himself. He was moving away as fast as his legs could carry him. He however, resisted the temptation to run. It was too early to take that risk. He got to the provision store, stood briefly pretending to price the cigarette. His lips were shaking. The words coming out of his mouth were low and meaningless. The sleeping sales boy was still snoring and probably dreaming of Murvi's visit.

Murvi saw that he was quiet far away from the gate. A distance far enough to break loose. All spectators were gazing on him from inside the gate. He bewildered them by bursting into a run and flew off at top speed. He was gone and out of sight before the gate was thrown open to let the crowd pursue him, it was too late.

The PMO regretted the silly mistake he made. He however, ordered the crowd to pursue him. The security men were reluctant to comply,but they had to obey before complain. The PMO led the crowd in chasing the crook, but in vain. They couldn't trace him. The PMO had no one to blame, but himself. He learned a lesson that the tricks of crook are many.

Timbo town had only one main street. From the hospital, the street went through the market square and the police station to the chief's palace where it ended. The street was lined

on both sides with shady trees. The trees were planted at intervals of five meters apart. The street was perfuriated on both
sides by many tributaries of narrow bushy footpaths branching
off it and leading to other parts of the town. Murvi sneaked off
the main street and he started running again through one of
the familiar footpaths. He knew that path was leading to where
people drank native liquor. Nobody noticed him branching off
through that path. With intense panic, the crook was fiercely
running and jumping over obstacles like big stones and fallen
logs on his way.

Unfortunately he totally forgot that there was a very big
hole of over four feet deep at a corner. That footpath had
grown very bushy. Many people had stopped passing through
it probably for fear of falling into the hole especially in the
night. Murvi soon found himself lying at the bottom of the
hole. It was almost a fatal fall. He unconsciously lay there with
a fractured right leg. He also had bruises in his thighs. Initially
Murvi only knew that he had fallen and no more.

He got to know of all the injuries he sustained, when he
came to his senses at Timbo hospital. The staff of the male
surgical ward were attending to him.

Five men had just closed from the native liquor area. They
were on their way home through the same footpath which
Murvi followed. It was not a mistake but a short cut to their
houses. They knew the road very well. The road was never a
trap for them. They saw Murvi unconscious at the bottom of
the familiar hole.

They quickly acted the good Samaritan. Murvi was carried
out of the hole and rushed to Timbo hospital. He was admitted at the male surgical ward. The PMO was being awaited
to attend to the new patient. All the nurses who admitted him
were ignorant of the fact that he was the thief being pursued

some moments ago. The five men who brought him couldn't give any clear history. They only said that he was found at the bottom of a deep pit along the path leading from the native beer parlour.

The PMO soon arrived, looking very pale and exhausted. Little did he know that his new patient was actually his wanted prey caught in a brand new net.

"What's the history?" the PMO asked.

"He was said to be coming back from a native liquor area. He fell into a deep pit and sustained all these injuries" the nurses narrated.

The PMO was amazingly gazing at the face lying in front of him. It looked familiar. He must have seen that face before probably not long ago. What puzzled him is the connection with the native drinking area. How could this man bear the same resemblance to Murvi the suspected thief. The PMO was battling with his memory.

"How comes that the story connects this man with a native liquor area?" he wondered. "Was this not the same face that played a nasty trick on me at the gate and ran away? Am I dreaming or what?" he had to prove his doubts. Any one coming from a beer parlour and falling into a deep pit, must have been drunk.

The doctor bent over and pushed his nose close to the patient's mouth under the pretext of examining his eyes. Actually he wanted to perceive the of odour of alcohol. Confirmed that there was no trace of it, his suspicion of the patient as being the wanted crook became greater. After all, he must have encountered his detrimental fate, consequent to his hurried escape. The PMO had to make more enquiries to be double sure.

"How do you know he was from a native beer parlour?" he asked the nurse on duty.

"These five men who brought him said so, doctor"

"Who is this man?" He turned to face the five men.

"We don't know him, doctor"

"How did you get him then?"

"We saw him in a pit when we were coming back from the native beer parlour. We were moved by compassion. We decided to bring him to the hospital as good Samaritans." One of them answered.

"At what time was it?"

The only one of the five who had a watch and was sensible enough to have looked at his watch when Murvi was rescued, answered,

"At about 1.15am, doctor"

The PMO quickly reflected in mind and came out with the calculation that it was about 15 minutes after Murvi broke loose. He was happy that his investigation was yielding positive result.

"Did any of you see this man at the beer parlour before you met him in this condition?"

"Yes doctor," answered one of the five at the surprise of the other four. That answer gave the doctor a little coldness in what he was getting at. Someone could go to the beer parlour without drinking. Furthermore, a fall is not always as a result of drunkenness.

It was however true that Murvi was at the beer parlour that night. Immediately he stole that money from the hospital,he passed through the said beer parlour before proceeding to his brother's house. He went to the drinking place not for alcohol but purposefully for pepper soup.

One woman usually cooks very nice and delicious cow tail pepper soup there. Murvi had once taken just a plate of that soup and wished he had more money to take more. Since then, he had a strong desire to satisfy his urge whenever he came across enough money. With over six hundred Naira in his hand he started salivating profusely with a higher desire to quench his taste. He had counted the money immediately he left the hospital and kept aside twelve naira for six plates of pepper soup and twenty naira for drinks that night.

Unfortunately, when he got to the pepper soup joint, he met someone finishing the last plate of it that evening. That was one of the five men who recognized him in the hospital. Murvi had looked piteously disappointed when he missed his desire. The man had observed that and offered to share the remaining portion of his plate of soup with Murvi.

Failing to satisfy the first priority of his desires at the beer parlour, Murvi automatically lost appetite for all things including beer. He straightaway left for his junior brother's house. From there he went back to the hospital where he became a centre of attraction.

The PMO wondered at the positive answer of the man who knew Murvi. How could that man who was with them at the gate, some few moments ago, be seen at the beer parlour almost at the same time.

"Could this man be a mysterious person? However, let me dig more. The rat could still be cornered" he contemplated.

"Do you mean you were drinking with him this night before fate decided his condition?"

"No, he didn't stay long at the beer parlour. It appeared to me that his main purpose was to take pepper soup. Failing to get it, he left almost immediately. He seemed to have been in a very great hurry."

"At what time was it please?"

"It was around 9.30pm doctor"

The doctor threw his memory into work again. He quickly

realized that the given time fell within the period Murvi initially ran off with the stolen government revenue.

"Thank you" the doctor remarked. "The real truth will soon come to light."

"What do you mean doctor?" one of the five men asked. He was afraid that the doctor might be suspecting them for foul play.

"I mean this man will soon come back to life to tell us the true version"

"Do you think we have something to do with his calamity doctor?" one of the five men asked.

"No, not at all. Infact, all of you deserve a noble prize for your excellent generosity."

"But what makes you think we have not told you the whole truth?" Asked another one of the five.

"Not that you have not told the truth. All you know is the fact that you met this man at the bottom of a deep hole. You pitied his condition and rushed him to this hospital isn't it?"

"Yes doctor", they all echoed.

"You see? To establish an acceptable history of this sick man, we have to know what happened immediately before, during and soon after the calamity befell him. You have told me part of the story. The remaining portions will have to be told by the patient himself."

"What if he dies, doctor?"

"He wouldn't die. He has just fainted from the shock of the heavy fall. His heart beat is still high, within the range of a normal living creature."

Murvi remained unconscious for quite a long time. At last, he started shaking his head and the limbs. Soon his eyes started opening to see things. He first of all looked straight to the ceiling. He wondered where he was. From the ceiling, his eyes moved to the walls of the ward. They later fell on the lines of the bed with human bodies either lying or sitting on them in different positions. Finally his eyes met with the curious faces of the men and women standing around him. He recognized the P.M.O straight away. It was only then he knew he was in the hospital once more. He tried to move his legs but discovered that one of them couldn't just move and was paining seriously. The other leg was also painful but not as much.

He started to recollect all the episodes of that night. His mind went to the way he got away with government revenue in the first place; his missing pepper soup at the beer parlour; the brief talk he had with his junior brother; his return to the hospital; the fight he had with the security men; the saving trick he played at the gate and finally his escape at top speed. He started to guess the cause of the calamity that brought him back to the hospital. He must have fallen after breaking loose from the gate and hurt his legs. He recognized the man who volunteered to share part of his plate of pepper soup with him. He wondered why that man was in the hospital. He suddenly began to groan as he felt the sharp pains on his legs.

"Haww... oommed chi. My legs", he said with difficulties. He attempted to move his legs again but the P.M.O cautioned him not to do so. Gazing at the PMO once more, Murvi knew he was already in for trouble.

"This is surely the man who fell a victim of my cunny trap at the gate", he thought.

The P.M.O waited until the patient recovered fully from the panic of discovering where he was before interrogating him.

# CHAPTER EIGHTEEN

# A DANGEROUS BAIL

"WHAT IS YOUR NAME?" the PMO asked the patient.

"I am known as Salami" Murvi answered. It was not a lie. That was the name he was given by his grandmother. She seemed to be the only one who was calling him by that name.

"Is that the only name you have?"

"I am also called Naryip together with my father's name; Vi". He was once more right. However, the name most wanted by the doctor was "Murvi" which actually means the son of Vi. Being the first son of his father, he was most popularly called Murvi by the villagers.

"Have you seen those men before?" the doctor asked, pointing to the five men.

"No, not at all", Murvi replied. "I only know that one", he pointed to the man who gave him a share of his pepper soup.

"How did you come to know him?"

"I met him this evening at the beer parlour. He was kind to me. He opted to share his plate of pepper soup with me."

"A corresponding answer" the doctor contemplated.

"Do you know me?" the doctor continued with Murvi.

"Yes"

"How"

"You were the one who examined and admitted my aunt for medical care."

"Sure this must be the wanted Murvi", the doctor assured himself and asked further, "you are right and you are the one that woman calls Murvi. Isn't it?"

"Yes, I am the one, doctor."

"I see, but why didn't you say so in the first place?"

"My name is not actually Murvi, but my aunt calls me so, meaning the son of Vi."

Murvi tried to move his thickly bandaged leg but it was not possible. He groaned once more in great pain. He glanced at the P.M.O and the other spectators again. He saw a conspicuous change in the P.M.O's face immediately he confirmed that his name was Murvi. It was only then that he also confirmed the P.M.O was the one who saw him escape at the gate.

"Unfortunately I have fallen back into the very trap I cunningly tried to avert." Murvi started contemplating deeply. "I thought the tricks had saved me, but fate had her grip on me. Here I am being at the mercy of the finger I tried to bite."

On the other hand, the P.M.O was thanking his stars. He has confirmed beyond doubt that the wanted crook was helplessly in his hands. He wouldn't allow Murvi to know that he was a suspect. He thanked the five good Samaritans and begged them to go home and rest. He was himself very tired and must also go home to rest. He called the ward incharge and cautioned him to keep an eye on Murvi.

That nurse was the only one to whom the P.M.O revealed Murvi's true identity. He was told that Murvi was the suspect in that Fibina's lost revenue issue. He was specifically warned never to do a thing that will cause Murvi to imagine anything fishy about his identity.

The ward incharge was John. He was good at carrying out orders. He called all his ward staff and issued the following orders to them:

(i)     That patient called Naryip on bed 12 is a special one.

(ii)    We must give him great attention

(iii)   At no time should he be taken out without the company of a male attendant

(iv)    No relative of his, should be allowed to sign him out against medical advice.

(v)     No mistakes, please. The P.M.O has a special interest in Naryip's case.

One of the ward attendants had overheard the P.M.O's talk to John. He knew exactly why Murvi was to be given such a special attention. He automatically developed special excitement. There was the possibility that Murvi still had the stolen government revenue intact. The attendant called Segun was left bewildered. He wondered why the P.M.O decided to leave Murvi unsearched till later. Was it not better for the suspect to be searched straight away despite his calamity? Segun was anxious. He wanted to make sure Murvi had the said sum of money on him. He was interested in it.

The general state of austerity in the country was very serious. It had eaten deep into the heart of every body especially civil servants. Prices of commodities had risen beyond the reach of low-incomed citizens. Junior civil servants like Segun were serious victims of the hard time. They were easily recognized in the society.

Most of them like Segun, had very mighty heads lying on tiny long necks. Their small sunken eyes, made them look like malnourished sick baboons.

The bases of their necks were deeply pressed in, exposing the ends of the clavicle bones. Their limbs were just mere skinny bones without flesh. Their stomachs bulged out like pregnant women, but their buttocks were hardly visible. Generally, they appeared like disfigured tiny human beings without buttocks.

Despite the hard pinch of the austerity measures, it appeared people like Segun always had enough money for drinking alcohol, but none for food. Segun had almost forgotten what lunch and dinner meant but remembered only breakfast and hangover. The credit for remembering breakfast went to his wife.

His wife usually forced him to take a bite of food every morning in the name of breakfast. That was however the only meal for the day to the family. The only member of the family who had extra feeding during the day was Segun. The extra food for Segun was alcohol. He always comes back home very late in the night and completely drunk. His wife always wondered where Segun got money for drinking but had never provided any for the family's feeding. The source of money for the meager morning meal for the family, was totally from the sweats of his wife. She toiled all day buying and re-selling vegetables and grains with very meager gains. She saw no benefit in her husband calling himself a civil servant.

Segun had never taken home any part of his salary. The salaries were usually very late sometimes in arrears of two or more months' delay. He was always in serious debts, mainly caused by over drinking on credit. His salary was only two hundred and fifty Naira, per month. For that month, Segun was indebted to the tune of five hundred and seventy naira.

Segun had longed for an opportunity to knock it's way to him. An opportunity to enable him clear all his debts. Such opportunities seem to have eluded him for long. His mind went to the patient with fractured leg called murvi

"Could it be true that the poor creature lying helpless on bed 12 , might be in possession of over six hundred naira ?" he asked himself. A thought flash through his mind that it could be the long awaited opportunity at his disposal. He started contemplating deeply.

"Is that money not said to be government revenue, which is actually nobody's money?" he thought. "Is that not the free for all money which dubious opportuned people, make away with, through the tricks of ink and pen? When shall I ever become one of them to eat my own share of the cake? That helpless creature is likely harbouring my own luck. I only hope and pray that those five good Samaritans were not smart enough to call it their share. Infact, I wouldn't forgive them if actually they have re-stolen the government revenue away from Murvi." Segun became restless. He moved up and down, focusing his attention on Murvi. He however decided to build up hope. After all , good Samaritans can not be bad at the same time. They can not be saving life and at the same time robbing the person. Suddenly, John called him.

"Sir", Segun answered.

"It's almost 4.00am", John said.

"Come and hold this patient up for his injection", John was standing near the bed 12 on which Murvi lay with a fractured leg. Segun was glad that it was an opportunity for him to confirm his thoughts.

"I am coming Sir", Segun said and ran to meet John. As he tried to hold Murvi up, he tactically felt the patient's trouser pocket. He touched some bundles of paper notes.

"Surely he has them", Segun thought.

"Who says it is not the long awaited opportunity for me? There is a saying that opportunity knocks only once. You either catch it as it comes or miss it forever", Segun was thrown into a deep thought.

"After clearing my debts, I don't care leaving government work. After all, how much do I derive from it? The meagre salary I earn as a civil servant, usually enticed me into huge debts. It lures me into drinking on credit, womanizing on credit, getting myself dressed on credit and a host of other essential things that I do or get on credit. At last, I am left with nothing out of the meagre salary to carry home, except carrying over of the debts to the next month. I am tired of such useless vicious cycle in life. I could join my wife to sell vegetables or grains in the market. By the way isn't it her occupation that keep my family faintly alive? With me to assist her, our life condition may become better. My hope of clearing the debts in the first place is the wonderful opportunity that Murvi has brought to me. I have only two hours left for this opportunity to elude me. I must do something and do it fast." Segun said and started meditating on how to get the money from Murvi.

Segun kept a small box in which he stored many varieties of drugs. The drugs were his collections from left overs by inpatients after discharge. He quickly ran to the box hidden behind a cupboard. He removed something from it and hurried to Murvi's bedside. He had about ten minutes discussion with Murvi. Finally he was able to convince Murvi to take three tablets of valum at once. He said the tablets were for pain relief.

Unfortunately for Murvi and fortunately for Segun, Murvi soon fell into a deep sleep. All patients around were sleeping. John was busy at his table writing reports. His view to Segun and Murvi was covered by a blue curtain separating his table from the rest of the ward. As soon as Murvi slept off, Segun wasted no time. He quickly searched him and made away with the said sum of money. He was still pocketing the money with panic striken hands, when one of the patients groaned deeply, Segun was frightened to death. His eyes bulged out and his whole body stiffened for sometime. He relaxed again when Segun realized that the patient was ignorant of his dubious action.

Unfortunately, Segun's action was tantamount to a dangerous bail.

# CHAPTER NINETEEN

## SEGUN'S SINCERE CONFESSION

IT WAS DAYBREAK. Segun was uneasy. He had to wait until 6..45am when the morning duty staff would come to take over from them. Unknown to Segun and the other night duty staff, the PMO had taken the case to the police. The security men carefully considered the case to establish their line of action. Yes, Murvi is the prime suspect. However, there are possibilities that he didn't take the money. Fibina might have played an intelligent trick to get away with it. Even if Murvi made away with the money; the likelihood of other people snatching it from him cannot be ruled out completely. The men who took him to the hospital are good suspects too. Others are the P.M.O himself, all the night duty staff in the male surgical ward, all the patients and their relatives in that ward and even the three security men who fought with him cannot be left out. The search of sister Fibina will have to go along with all the evening shift staff of the female medical ward. It might go down to the patients of that ward and their relatives as well. After thoroughly considering the case, the armed security men decided to start the search with the male surgical ward. It was a wise decision since the prime suspect was on admission there.

The armed policemen took their position at 6.00am, sealing the whole hospital premises. Some of them went straight to the male surgical ward. Segun and other night shift staff of that ward, were preparing to handover to those on morning shift,

105

suddenly, they saw some armed policemen appearing. All the staff were ordered to stand still where ever they were in the ward without movement. None of the morning duty staff of that ward was allowed to go in.

One of the policemen proceeded to bed twelve. Murvi was still battling with the effect of the heavy dose of valum given to him by Segun in the early hours of the morning. The policeman started searching him thoroughly while the others kept an eye on all other suspects. John, Segun, the other night duty staff, patients and their relatives were to keep still. No movements, no talking, no body movements or signs of any kind to one another. Segun was sweating despite the cold weather of that morning. He knew the accounting time had come. He didn't know what to do at all. He felt like melting into thin air. No way out. He was surely in for it. His neck was in for the slaughter in the place of Murvi the initial culprit. He was panic stricken and his limbs were vibrating. Segun was praying that the search should only end with Murvi.

"I wonder what reason they will give for searching the staff too." Segun hopelessly thought. He therefore had a slight relief from the unbearable tension in him. He vainly hoped that he might escape the hook after all.

The search team were soon over with all the patients and their relatives. The suspected money was not found on them. They turned their eyes to the staff. All the staff were to quickly line up behind John, the staff nurse incharge.

Segun started scratching his head, wiping his face and squeezing his fingers unconsciously. He had wrapped the stolen government money in a plolythene bag and stocked it into his pants.

"Oh God!" Segun exclaimed. "Where on earth would I go? Why did I get myself entangled into this stupid mess of a bone fractured foolish thief? What I thought was the long awaited good opportunity has turned out to be the worst. I might end up loosing the expected opportunity and be left with my work also at stake, my future at stake, my personality gone, my family in disgrace, and all what not, count it."

He actually started praying. He prayed in tongues, not aloud but in mind. He dared not open his mouth to the hearing of the search team. He was casting out the demons of temptation, the Lucifer of greed, the dragons of fear, the vampires of poverty, the temptations of drunkenness, the polluted systems of the civil service, the bad spirits of pride and all other demons that led him into the horrible action.

Unfortunately, it appeared the demons were stubborn. Segun was still gripped by an unbearable fear. He felt like urinating. He was in the middle of the line of staff waiting to be searched. A female ward attendant was at his back. The painful pressure of the urine trying to come out was unbearable. He wanted to visit the toilet, but they were not supposed to move without permission. He tried hard to attract the attention of the policemen to him. He was obliged to raise his hand several times but no one noticed him. He couldn't shout to beg for excuse because they were not to talk nor make noise at all. To run off to the toilet without permission was surely a detrimental act that could aggravate suspicion. It could even lead someone to be roughly malhandled by the policemen.

The pressure became too much for Segun. He couldn't bear it any longer. He raised both hands and started waving them vigorously over his head from side to side. Luckily for him, one of the policemen noticed his action and moved towards him. Unfortunately, the waste liquid couldn't wait for formalities. Before the security man got to Segun, the liquid forced its way out. Wetting its way through Segun's pair of trousers, the warm liquid ran down his lap and formed a pole on the floor. He knew what was happening. He was left with a bewildered gaze at the back of the person infront of him on the queue.

The female attendant behind Segun, saw the pole of urine on the floor. She was obliged to push the line backwards. A gap was made between Segun and herself. She was almost chuckling herself with surging laughter. She remembered a quarrel she once had with Segun. This man had called her a good for nothing harlot. An abuse she would never forget. She had no power to fight back. She considered the shameful display which has now put Segun in a public disgrace and said in her mind, "That serves him right. Surely the gods have come to avenge me".

The policeman got to Segun. He enquired, what the matter was. Segun was dumbfounded, he couldn't speak. The security man's attention was drawn to the floor. This was due to the way the female attendant was looking. He saw the urine which was forming a map shape. He straightaway understood Segun's problem. He beckoned Segun out of the queue and escorted him to the toilet. Every body in the ward saw him dashing into the toilet with wet trousers. All of them burst out laughing despite the order for silence. The female attendant laughed loudest and she was the last to stop laughing.

Nobody actually suspected that the money could be with Segun. They all counted it as one of those unfortunate embarrassments in life, especially when one is kept under undue pressure. The security men were to carry the whole blame.

Sergent Fesus Moniva, was the only one who linked Segun's disgraceful act to a sign of internal guilt. Fesus was the man who escorted Segun to the toilet. He therefore decided to interview him as soon as they entered the private room.

"What is your name man?" Fesus began

"My name is Segun Joba sir," Segun answered. He was trying to unbutton his trousers. His hands were shaking as he did so. If he had the slightest chance, Segun would have dropped the money into the toilet pit. It meant nothing to him at that time. Unfortunately, Fesus kept a strict eye on him. He saw that Segun actually wore a conspicuously guilty look.

"Segun",

"Sir",

"Do you have something to confess?"

"Yes Sergeant."

"What is it?"

"I must confess that I find it difficult to pass stool whenever someone is watching me."

"Shut up", Fesus said furiously.

"What of passing urine when hundred pairs of eyes are watching you?"

"I am sorry sergeant, but it wasn't my fault. I was disgraced as a result of trying to obey your orders."

"Be serious and don't waste my time please. I have a duty to watch all your actions, including your so called passing stool. If you think my presence will hinder you from easing yourself, then lets go back to the ward."

Segun saw that there was no way out. He therefore decided to make a true confession to the sergent.

"I have another confession to make please."

"What again?"

"I am afraid to say it"

"Afraid of what? Feel free Segun. I could be of help to you, if the confession is sensible."

"Oh sergeant! I am really scared but can I rely on you?"

"Absolutely. Why not be fast and brief."

"Alright, hear my sincere confession." Segun said. He

quickly put his hand into his pant and drew out a black poly-thene bag. The content appeared thick and slightly heavy. He handed it to sergeant Fesus who was curiously gazing at it.

"What is in the bag?"

"You are free to open it sir. That is nothing, but my sincere confession."

Fesus bravely opened the bag. He nodded his head at what he saw, "Unbelievable!", he exclaimed as he gazed at the packed twenty Naira notes mixed with some ten and five Naira notes. He quickly counted them and saw that they totaled the said sum of money, which had been stolen. Murvi had not spent anything from it yet.

"Surprised" Fesus exclaimed again.

"Do you mean you were the one who stole the Government Revenue?"

"No, Sergeant. I am a second hand thief."

"What do you mean?"

"It's quite clear, Sergeant. Murvi is the first thief. Yesternight, I bought his rank at a great price to become the second hand thief."

"I am still at a lost. Come out clearly and explain yourself please."

"O.K here you are. Murvi stole the money from the female medical ward. In an attempt to escape justice, he fell and had a fractured leg. That calamity pulled him back into the net he wanted to avoid. He now lies sick on bed 12 in this ward. I foolishly thought it was my luck to have the money. Consequently, I drugged him yesternight and made away with it and ended up soaking my trousers with urine out of fear. This earned me the greatest disgrace on earth. With you watching all my steps and the search awaiting me in the ward, I see no way out."

"Now I understand, but what do you expect me to do for you?"

"I don't mind Sergeant, If you would like to become the third hand fellow please. Bail me out as I bailed Murvi, if you can."

"I am sorry, Segun, my profession prohibits that kind of game. I must keep to my oath of office."

"Wha.........aaaat?" Segun was terrified at the answer.

"I surely mean what I said. You are just in for it. I only wish justice be fair to you for your true confession."

"You are a unique sergeant. I wish every other person including myself were to keep to their oath of office in this country."

The sergeant pocketed the money in his trouser pocket and handcuffed Segun. He showed little or no resistance at all. The sergeant escorted him out of the toilet. Unfortunately the sergeant forgot that the bottom of his trouser pocket was open.

# CHAPTER TWENTY

# SULE PICKED HIS LUCK

EVERYBODY IN THE WARD was surprised to see Segun coming out of the toilet with both bound together. The police officer incharge of the search was wondering why Fesus and Segun delayed much in the toilet. Seeing Segun in handcuff, he understood and asked Fesus for no explanations. Everybody concluded that Segun was the victim of that search. The uncontrolled urine passed publicly by Segun, was straight away attributed to the fear of getting caught. John and all the night duty staff, began wondering how Segun got involved.

"How did you fish him out?" The officer incharge asked.

Confidently, Fesus narrated the whole story of their long stay and the dialogue they had in the toilet.

The excitement of catching the culprit, made Fesus not to notice that the money was no longer in his pocket. Immediately Fesus recovered the money from Segun, he pocketed it into his right side trouser pocket. Unfortunately, that side of the pocket was opened at the bottom. He forgot that he had burnt open that side of the pocket with a very hot pressing iron.

It all happened when he was hurriedly pressing his uniform to use it for an important duty. Fesus knew about it, but he kept forgetting to mend it.

The money lingered in Fesus' pocket only for a short time. It soon made its way down on the toilet floor unnoticed by Fesus. It dropped at the door just when they were opening it to go out. The door was the type that made a lot of noise at opening and closing. The money fell off just near the door but inside the room. The noise made by the door must have contributed to Fesus not noticing when the money dropped.

"You mean you have recovered the money and it is now with you?" the officer asked.

"Yes Sir", Fesus answered without checking his pockets.

"Have you counted and confirmed the amount?"

"I did Sir."

"Weldone sergeant, You have lessened our work." The officer commended. There is no need to waste anymore time. Let's take this idiot to the P.M.O's office. As for that crook on bed 12, I will detail some smart boys to keep an eye on him."

The door was finally opened to the morning duty staff to enter the ward as the night duty staff were released.

Sule, one of the morning duty ward attendants was the first to enter the toilet after the exit of Segun and Fesus.

He was a short and fat man, dark in complexion. His short legs stood on swollen feet typical of people with elephantiasis.

His toes were almost all of the same size, very short with invisible joints. He has never worn a cover shoe because he had never found the size that fits his feet. His head was comparatively small with big bulging eyes and very thick lips. His huge oversized ears looked out of place. People hate to see Sule smile due to the bad odour that usually emanate from his mouth. His teeth were thickly coated with continuous food deposits having yellow colour of decay. Only God knows when Sule last brushed his teeth. When asked why he doesn't brush his teeth, he would laugh and shamelessly say the thick coat acted as a gum to keep his teeth together.

"Without the gummy coat, my teeth will part to pieces" he usually said.

Sule went into the toilet not to ease himself, but to sweep it. He was very good at his duties. The male surgical ward was graded as the neatest of all the wards in Timbo Hospital. Most of the credit went to Sule's dedication to his duties.

Unfortunately, Sule was one of those people who could not see money and leave it. He never steals, but any loose money with no clear ownership coming across him, became his own. As long as there was a slight doubt as to whether or not he had it, no Jupiter can force him to release it.

Sule was once confronted by Sergent Fesus Moniva. The policeman who escorted Segun to the toilet room.The confrontation took place in a beer parlour. Sule was provoked by one harlot.The harlot drunkenly entered the beer parlour and jokingly snatched a stick of cigarette from Sule who was not in a mood for jokes. He angrily snatched his stick of cigarette back and rewarded the woman with a dirty slap in her face. She screamed as if she was going to die the next minute.

Just then, Fesus one of her boy friends came in. He was told of what happened. He took Sule with the harlot aside and started raining abuses and all types of dangerous threats at Sule. Though he was in a civilian dress, Sule knew he was a policeman so he dared not retaliate. Any utterance from him could lead to his getting accused of different crimes you can think of. Talking to one policeman could mean abusing the whole police force. It could also mean disturbing public peace. Count it, a host of other dangerous crimes, which the policemen could decide to label on him. However, he inwardly wished Fesus the worst of all lucks. He hated Fesus since then and also wished he could one day be chanced to revenge.

As soon as Sule bent down to sweep the toilet floor, he was taken aback by what he saw.

"Am I dreaming or is it real?" he contemplated. He bent

down lower to touch the bundles of twenty Naira notes. "These are real" he said. I am not dreaming. But how did this money come in here?"

He was not aware of the missing money case. None of the morning shift staff who were locked out during the search, knew anything about it. Most of them thought the policemen had brought in a sick criminal. Others thought the night duty staff must have committed a serious crime which warranted their interrogation.

Sule who was also locked out did not even care to enquire what was going on. He went about his outdoor normal duties. He had seen his enemy Fesus among the search team and he didn't want to have a second look at him. He was busy picking up dirty pieces of rags and papers around..

Immediately the door was opened to them, Sule rushed in with his broom to the toilet to continue his work. Ignorantly, he couldn't link his findings at the toilet to what went wrong.

Sule picked up the bundles of money notes. He counted them and was surprised. He pushed aside a black polythene bag which was lying on the floor, with the hope of finding more. It was a bit heavy; he picked it up and saw that one more bundle was left in it. He removed the bundle and jointly counted them all.

"This is my salary for four months and yet someone decided to play about with it." He said with a smile. "This must have been dropped by one of the rich relative of patients or probably the patient themselves."

"None of the hospital staff could boast of such an amount now. None, not even the P.M.O, especially now that the month is far reaching the end."

Sule was trying hard to figure out how the money came into the toilet. He was tired of exhausting his brain.

"To hell with who dropped it", he exclaimed at last. "Miracles could still happen. God is a wonderful Being. He knows the poor and the rich. He knows that I am the poorest of all cleaners in this hospital. He knows I needed some money today. He knows my wife is soon going to deliver. He knows that the hospital authorities have no mercy even to poor staff like me. He knows my two children are soon going back to school and I must settle all their requirements. He knows my house is leaking very badly and it requires urgent repairs", Sule was counting all his problems known by God who has provided the solution to them. He burst out into a deep-hearted smile.

"Oh Allah! You are good.Thank you God. Thank you …..o."

Suddenly there was a knock at the door. Sule was interrupted in his showers of praises to God. He was confused. He didn't know what to do with the money vibrating in his hand. However, he had to do something to gain time. He straight away pretended to be passing stool.

"Hiilmah! Hiiii mmmmah" Sule began to push hard and loud like a pregnant woman under labour. There was a knock again.

"Jo… uuust a-a-a-a-a mminute pillease .." Sule was pretentiously pleading as if under hard struggle. He was pleading for the person at the door to give him just a minute.

The brief trickish time he gained, was enough for him to cook up an idea. He could make use of the dirty dustbin. Yes, a good idea. He quickly wrapped the money with the polythene bag and buried it deep into the dirt in the dustbin. It was his habit to carry the dust bin to wherever he went to sweep.

Having made sure that the money was well covered by the dirts in the dustbin, he stopped his fake labour exercise. He felt relaxed. He then proceeded to the door and opened it.

Fesus the policeman pushed in and looked straight into Sule's face. He saw him holding a broom in one hand and the other hand holding his stomach.

"I am sorry, Sir", Sule pleaded.

"Hope I have not delayed you much. I was disturbed by a serious diarrhea." he lied. He was speaking boldly without any sign of fear or guilt except signs of pains in his stomach.

Fesus recognized Sule straight away. He knew the type of person Sule was. Imagining the type of enemity that existed between them, he felt cold blood rushing down his backbone.

"No hope", Fesus uttered in mind.

"This crook is the king of all crooks. Even if he has the money, as long as there is a slight doubt about his picking it, no torture on earth could make him release it." Fesus was battling with that thought while gazing suspiciously at Sule. Sule was not happy at the way he was looking at him.

"Don't you want to use the toilet?" Sule asked. "Bye the way, what is the matter sergent? You seemed prepared to swallow me alive with your eyes. Permit me to ask whether it is a fresh issue or you still hate to see me? Are you still harbouring that old time issue? If you don't want to use the toilet, you may wish to excuse me to sweep the toilet please". Sule ended his long talk.

Fesus thought of the answer he gave to his boss. He had publicly agreed that he had collected the money from Segun. He has to play it cool with Sule. Luck may still fall his way to recover the money.

"Please Sule" he pleaded. "Let us forget of the past. I had long forgotten about that unfortunate incident. It surprises me why you still harbour this in your mind. You know very well where it occurred. Beer parlour is a devilish place. A place where the best of friends get into serious conflicts.

Consequently, dangerous quarrels and even fight may occur. Do we blame them? No, blame alcohol, the devil. Let us forget the past and be friends please"

"It appears you are not pressed to use the toilet"

"No, I am not"

"Then, what are you here for?"

"I have a pressing problem which requires your kind cooperation, please"

"A pressing problem?" Sule wondered.

"Indeed, Sule. I very much count on your generous cooperation please."

"What do you mean sergeant? Do you want me to join you in the problem or you are requesting me to solve the problem for you?"

"I am begging you to solve the problem for me please"

"Are you serious, sergeant?"

"I am very much serious"

"Who deceived you that I have experience in police duties to solve your problem, sergeant? You know I am just a common ward cleaner who knows nothing except cleaning in and outside the ward. Who am I to solve a problem encountered by a whole police sergeant? By the way, what is the problem in the first place?"

"Thank you Sule. Your last question makes sense" Fesus was glad. "Are you aware of the confusion in this ward which led to the intervention by the security men? You know it ended up with the arrest of ........." Fesus was still speaking when Sule interrupted him.

"Well, I saw Segun being escorted out with both hands in chain, but the details I have none. Were you not the one who took him out of the ward?"

"Yes, I was"

"Then what details do you expect from me better than what you already know? I had no time to ask around for the details due to the crowded nature of my job"

"Please Sule, your imaginations are still far off, from the real problem. I beg you to allow me land before you come in please." Fesus pleaded cautiously, not to hurt Sule's mind.

"Alright sergeant. Just hit the nail straight on the head please"

"Good. Here we are." Fesus said almost hurriedly. I was with Segun in this toilet some minutes ago. The sum of six hundred and fifty naira fell off my pocket right here. It is suspected to be government revenue. I have come to look for it". He went straight to the point.

"I see." Sule nodded his head.

"I now understand why you need my help."

"Yes Sule, that's all." Fesus said with slight hope.

"Over six hundred naira is not small money to joke with. I must surely give you my fullest cooperation sergeant. Are you sure it dropped out right here in the toilet?"

This was however, a million naira question to answer. Actually he wasn't exactly sure where the money had fallen off. It could have fallen in the toilet room, along the dark corridor leading to the P.M.O.'s waiting room. Fesus got to know that the money was lost, right in the P.M.O.'s office. He couldn't produce it when he was asked to.

"Frankly speaking Sule, the toilet room is just one of the possible places where the money could have dropped"

"It's a pity sergeant." Sule said, but he was glad that no one could point a clean suspicious finger at him. It was still in doubt whether or not the money dropped in the toilet.

"Lets us not waste any more time. Sule" Fesus suggested.

"I agree"

"Then answer me. Did you see any money in the toilet here or not?"

"I just came to sweep . I haven't started yet. The diarrhea really disturbed me. Since you were in this toilet some moments ago, you can bear me witness that nothing has changed so far." Fesus sensed that he was running out of his last straw of hope. The best he can do is to recollect himself and act as a policeman should. He saw that the toilet was not swept yet, but that doesn't rule out the possibility of Sule coming across the money. He must act fast.

"I have to search you Sule" Fesus said at last. "any objection?"

"No, but are you suspecting me?" Sule boldly asked."

"Who else, when you have been found alone in one of the likely places the money could have fallen off."

"Alright, but I have to establish some witnesses for my being searched innocently. I thought you needed my cooperation to help you find the money. If you are however suspecting me to have stolen it, I must go to any length to prove that I am not a thief. I am sure policemen are not above the law of defamation of character". Sule said furiously.

"Look Sule"Fesus replied. "Nobody has called you a thief. I like people who look serious, sincere and innocent like you, but our country is very difficult to understand. It is very difficult to know the real sincere ones from the fake ones. The real innocent ones can not be easily separated from the fake innocent ones. Consequently, you can't blame me for the decision to search you."

"As you wish, but I only said I want to establish witnesses, that's all."

"What do you suggest?"

"Let's go to my boss, Mr. Sam, if you insist to search me please."

"Come on, let's go." Fesus was determined.

The nursing Superintendent (NS) in-charge of the ward was surprised to see them enter his office. At first, he thought the investigation of Segun in the PMOs' office had involved Sule. He wondered how Sule got himself entangled into the case, but he gave them chance to explain.

"Excuse me NS". The policeman started. "You may be surprised why I am back to this ward"

"Surely, I am" Sam said

What is it again?

"I collected some money from Segun, suspected to be the stolen government money. That money is lost now. I suspected that it must have fallen in one or two places including your ward toilet. I went straight to that room to look for it and met this man there. I suspected he must have picked the money. I wanted to search him but he insisted that the action be done in your presence. That is why we are here."

"Do you know the nature of his work?" Sam asked.

"Yes he is a ward orderly who keeps the ward clean."

"That's right sergeant and that includes cleaning the toilet too" Sam said.

"Yes, I know all that, but is that enough reason to exculpate him from the allegation?"

"Well sergeant, I have no objection to what you intend to do, but I have my doubts." The N.S said

The sergeant sensed an element of conspiracy between Sule and his boss. He almost lost his temper, but he decided to take it cool .He was determined to search Sule.

He ordered Sule to raise his hands above his head. He searched him properly. He started massaging him all over and was putting his hand into Sule's uniform pockets one after the other. At a point, he ordered Sule to un- button his trousers and shake it up and down. Sule wanted to resist that order but the N.S cautioned him to obey all instructions "Let him clear all doubts, Sule", Sam said. Sule obeyed the voice of his boss. In the process of carrying out the last order, sule had to expose his pants. It was very dirty, appearing not to have been put into water for years. The breath breaking odour that radiated from the pant was too strong .Sam and the policeman could not stand it. They tactifully raised their palms to their mouth to avoid the odour. "So this man is completely rotten from mouth to bottom" the NS thought. "Is this actually the man who is supposed to maintain cleanliness?" the sergeant thought.

After thoroughly searching Sule to no avail, Fesus was seriously disappointed and discouraged.

"I hope you are now satisfied that the money is not with this poor fellow officer", Sam asked.

"It really appears so and I am really very sorry for the inconveniences caused" Fesus replied hopelessly.

Sule almost burst out with joy hoping that the money is save for him in the dust bin.

"Did you search the toilet properly before arresting this man?" Sam asked.

This questioned pricked Sule in his heart like a sharp needle. He inwardly hated Sam for it.

"I didn't have time to search the toilet because of the strong believe I had that the money could be with this man" Fesus replied.

"Then let us proceed there to make a thorough search. Luck may still be at your door", Sam suggested.

# CHAPTER TWENTY-ONE

## SULE'S DUST BIN

HEARING THE SUGGESTION BROUGHT BY SAM, Sule suddenly looked up. A strip of fear gripped his heart. He instantaneously hated his boss for the suggestion. Sule was afraid that a thorough search of the toilet at that moment, might include checking of the dustbin.

"Have you swept the toilet yet?" He asked Sule.

"No, not yet N.S" Sule replied. "I was about to start when the sergeant came."

"Now then, lets us go to the toilet room and clear all doubts", the N.S pressed on.

Sule almost trembled, but he cautioned himself to be sober for the avoidance of further suspicion.

"Don't betray yourself, Sule", he said to himself inwardly. "You have been brave so far, why not be a man up to the end- By the way the dustbin is full of filth. They may not even care to touch it" Sule felt relaxed.

The three proceeded to the toilet room. Sam and Fesus started to glance here and there in search of the money. Sule was not at ease. He was greatly worried, not because he feared the discovery of the money, but for the where about of his dustbin. He was the only one who noticed the disappearance of the dustbin. Sule only pretended to be looking for the missing money, when in the actual sense he was looking for the dustbin.

"Who must have visited the toilet and made away with

my treasure?" Sule wondered. He looked at the way Sam and Fesus were vainly gazing here and there. It appeared funny and stupid. Sule almost burst into laughter. Without the dustbin around, they would never find the money.

Back to the PMO's office, the police officer was worried why Fesus had delayed that much. From experience, he trusted Fesus, but the PMO did not. He couldn't believe Fesus's story of the broken pocket. He was ignorant of the fact that Fesus was rated as the most honest among his colleagues.

Fesus had just been in the police force for about four years, starting as a recruit, but he had rapidly risen to the rank of a full sergeant. His rapid promotion followed one act of honesty to the other. A good example is not far fetched.

One day Fesus was on the team of escorts to collect staff salary from the headquarters. On their way back, their vehicle was involved in a serious accident. Both the driver and the Cashier who were sitting in front of the car, were seriously injured. The other two police men who were with him at the back, were also left unconscious. All the injured men were hospitalized at a near by hospital.

Fesus was left alone to take care of the money which was about fifty million Naira. It was at last handed over to the station accountant. Unfortunately, when the money was counted, it fell short by twelve thousand. No doubt, all fingers pointed at Fesus.

He pleaded innocent, to no avail. Finally he was suspended indefinitely with half pay until twice the whole sum lost was recovered. Fesus who was innocent and had clear conscience, had to accept the penalty without blaming anyone but fate.

As luck would have it, it was discovered at the Bank headquarters that Timbo police station was underpaid by twelve thousand Naira during that month when Fesus fell victim.

Fesus was immediately recalled to work. He was paid the full arrears of the deducted part of his salary in double form. That was when he had his first promotion as an additional compensation for the wrong done to him. Many more acts of honesty, faithfulness and patience, earned Fesus the rapid promotions he enjoyed. Consequently,he was crowned with the mark of trust by all who knew him.

The police officer sent one of his men to go for Fesus. At last he came. His face was conspicuously depicting the greatest of all disappointments. He had openly accepted that he personally collected the said sum of money from Segun. He didn't know what to say or do, since the money was no where to be found.

"Haven't you seen the money?" the police officer asked.

"I haven't seen it, Sir", Fesus replied while saluting in their own way.

"Think twice Fesus. Did you actually collect the money from this crook?" The officer asked again.

Fesus started contemplating. "No use to reverse my statements", he thought "well, the truth is that I have not trickishly hidden the money. Wherever it is right now, God knows better. As usual, fate is the deciding factor". Fesus ended in deep thought.

"Yes Sir", he replied his boss. "I actually collected the money from him. I carefully counted and pocketed it."

The P.M.O thought Fesus was going to twist his answer, but to his utter surprise, Fesus was adamant.

"Did you say your pocket was burnt open by a hot pressing iron?", The P.M.O asked.

"Yes doctor."

"Can we see it please?" the doctor was not satisfied.

"Yes, why not", Fesus replied.

He pulled out his right trouser pocket and showed it to them. It had an open portion with burnt margins to confirm what Fesus said.

"It's a pity sergent, but the truth remains that the missing money has now been traced to you, isn't it?", the P.M.O said.

"Quite correct doctor, but the fact also remains that its actually not with me. Someone probably has it now, but fate destines me to carry the blame".

"Well, some facts are never facts but fakes in this country", the P.M.O thought. He turned to Segun and said, "as for you Segun, you have to face the music of dismissal straight away." Hearing this, Segun stooped and shook his head lamenting.

"And now I will really join my wife to buy and sell vegetables. Oh! God, can't there be a way out? I have really bailed Murvi out. I bought his penalty at a great price. If I had a forum, I want to tell my country that greediness is not good. I was greedy, but I ended up disappointed. The debt I intended to clear are still in my bones. In addition, I am now loosing the little source of income which if wisely used could clear the debts. Apart from greediness, chasing loose women and drunkenness are not wise practices. They ruined me, overworked my liver, stole my money for antibiotics, drained my blood and now my work is at stake. Oh! God! Help me, forgive me, rescue me and ...". His lamentations were interrupted by one of the policemen who shouted at him, got hold of his hand and pushed him out of the P.M.O's office. He escorted Segun to the ward to say his last goodbye. He was forced to handover all government properties in his possession. Finally, he left the ward, the hospital premises and the government umbrella. He was out into the wider world to face its horrible pinch, just for greediness. What a striking lesson!

After, Fesus was called by another policeman sent by his

boss, Sam also went to his office. Sule was left alone to continue his work. He swept the room at last but with a reluctant zeal. Though he was no longer interested in the money, he still had the urge to find out how the dust bin disappeared from the toilet room. He wanted to know whether the person who collected the dustbin, had discovered the money or not. If not, then what became of the money? Could it have been dropped into the garbage pit together with the dirt? Sule became restless "For the money to decay with the dirt, it were better if I had it", Sule wished himself hopelessly.

# CHAPTER TWENTY-TWO

# THE MYSTERIOUS MONEY

UNKNOWN TO SULE, Amina had seen him coming out of the toilet with Fesus. She saw them entering into Sam's Office. She was also a ward orderly. Since Sule came out empty handed, she knew Sule had left the dustbin in the toilet. Just then, one of the patients admitted in their ward, showed sign of wanting to vomit. Amina was standing near the said patient. She understood what the patient was trying to do. She had just swept and mopped the floor. Something had to be done quick to avoid the floor getting soiled too soon.

Amina ran into the toilet, brought out the dustbin and placed it in front of the patient to receive the vomit. The patient vomited into the bin. Amina picked up the container of filthy materials and carried it to the gabbage pit. She poured the whole content of the dustbin into the pit.

Unfortunately, the container also slipped from her hands and dropped into the deep hole. She screamed and rushed back to the ward to get help. She could have gotten Sule who was her co-worker in the same ward but to her dismay, Sule was still in the N.S office. She had to get help quick to rescue the dustbin for fear that it could get buried deeper down as more dirts came from other wards. The compound labourers were clearing grass around with the intention of gathering them into the pit as well. She decided to go for help from the next ward since Sule may delay longer.

She was running to the next ward when she suddenly met with the Principal Nursing Officer (P.N.O).

"Where are you running to, Amina?" The P.N.O asked.

"Anything wrong?" Amina stopped and started laughing.

"I want to go and call Philip from the next ward, Sir", Amina replied.

"What for?"

"To help me remove our dustbin from the garbage pit, Sir", she replied.

"You mean you dropped it into the pit?"

"Yes Sir, not intentional", she said with a quick smile.

"It mistakenly slipped from my hand and off it went, following the dirt"

"Where is Sule?"

"He is busy with the N.S, Sir"

"Well, therefore I have to make use of you",the P.N.O said.

"I want to send you to sister July's house in town. When you come back, you can continue with the exercise of rescuing your dustbin. We have an urgent Senior Staff Meeting today at 2.30pm. Please tell her to come and attend it unfailingly. Tell her that it is very crucial and her presence is very essential."

"Yes Sir", Amina obeyed and rushed off the hospital premises.

Sule didn't see Amina since the beginning of the morning session. He thought she was observing her day off. That was why he didn't even think of Amina in connection to the lost dustbin.

Jully's husband was the headmaster of Timbo Central Primary School. He had gone to the school. Jully had received an urgent letter from their son that morning. The son was a student in one secondary school, situated far away from Timbo town. In the letter, the son had requested the parents to send his school fees urgently, to enable him take the final year examination. Jully had rushed to the school to inform her husband about the letter.

Amina didn't meet her at home and so, she followed her to the school. She got there when Jully had just finished a discussion with her husband. She was trying to get back home when she met Amina.

"Hello, Amina, have you come to see me?", Jully said.

"Yes sister", Amina replied.

"The P.N.O sent me to tell you to come for an urgent Senior Staff Meeting at 2.30pm please." The two women were walking home together.

"How is the hospital, Amina?"

"Fine sister. The only new thing is that the Male Surgical Ward was filled with policemen this morning. All the night duty staff of that ward were lined up for searching one after the other. Finally, Segun the ward orderly was arrested."

"Tell me more, Amina. What did they do?"

"I don't know sister. They said it had something to do with Fibina's Case."

"Wonderful, you mean the case of the government revenue?"

"Exactly, sister. Even Sule seems to be involved as well."

"Really!!? How come that a problem in the Female Medical ward will go to affect staff of the Male Surgical Ward."

"My sister, that is the mystery. That crafty woman Fibina wants to get everyone hooked in her problems."

"I seem to agree with you, Amina. Just imagine or count the number of staff especially the junior ones who have got themselves entangled into that case of hers".

"Sister what can we say. You know we junior staff have no voice at all. Some of us are only working to keep soul and flesh together. It doesn't mean we are enjoying the job. People like Fibina will like us to carry the blame for their silly mistakes. Do you know that Segun was finally dismissed from work?"

"Segun dismissed?"

"Yes, Sister. He was given a few minutes to handover under pressure of an armed policeman."

"You mean the money was found on him?"

"No one is sure, sister. The policeman who arrested him had earlier confessed that he had recovered the money from Segun, but they came later looking for it again."

"What was his excuse please?"

"An unbelievable story sister. Just imagine a whole police sergent saying that the money dropped out of his pocket."

"What a mysterious money! In the first place, it was locked in a table drawer. Fibina said it disappeared from it. How it got to the stranger called Murvi and later Segun, only God knows. And now you are telling me that it jumped out of a policeman's pocket."

Amina burst into laughter and Jully joined her. Both laughed and laughed until they were tired.

"What puzzles me most is how Sule also came into the scene." Amina said under hard struggle as she was chuckling with laughter. As she did so, a small drop of saliva went into her trachea. She ended up coughing very seriously. Jully was only gazing at her helplessly and at last she said; "hardluck, Amina."

"Thank you" Amina replied. "I think that woman Fibina is a witch".

"What makes you say so?"

"Didn't you see what happened to me? I believe she must have overheard our conversation about her treacherous act. She wants to kill me through cough."

"You may be right, Amina. I heard that her first target, Murvi ended up with a fractured leg."

"And her second target Segun ended up loosing his job."

"You see!!" Both of them burst out laughing again.

"Let's hope that mysterious and dangerous drama doesn't get to us". Jully said at last.

"God forbid, sister. I must confess that I have never believed that money to be real. It always appeared to me that, only Fibina alone knows about the existence of that money."

"You may be right again, Amina, but what makes you think that way?"

"Because, it appears many innocent workers are getting involved ignorantly. A good example is Sule with whom I work in the same ward. How could he be involved when I can even swear on his behalf that he knows nothing about the case because we just came this morning to take over from the night duty staff. Surely he was as innocent as myself."

"That's true Amina. Don't be surprised that the case of Dr. Mali and Kimba; Mr. Kingsbay and Adini and a host of other calamities that befell some of our staff, may have their origin from Fibina's case."

The two women were approaching Jully's house. The time was getting to 11.00am. Amina suddenly remembered that the dustbin was still inside the deep gabbage pit.

"Come in Amina", Jully invited her to her house. "The sun is getting hot and you may wish to take a cup of cold water."

"Thank you, sister", Amina said. "I would have honoured your invitation, but I have a very urgent problem to solve at the hospital. Don't be offended, please permit me to go."

"What sort of problem is it, Amina? I hope it's not a secret."

"It's not a secret, sister, but it's a funny story."

"A funny story? Then let me have just a share of the fun. You need not go in, but just hint me right here at the door."

"It's about the new dustbin in our ward."

"You mean the one which Sule loves very much, isn't it? I always see him moving about with it in hand".

"Exactly that one sister."

"What about it Amina? I hope you didn't clash with him over it?"

"No, not at all. Sule left it in the toilet. He was escorted out to the N. S.' Office by an armed policeman. You know I told you that Sule seem to be in the net too. Suddenly, one seriously sick patient was about to vomit. That was just after I had swept and mobbed the floor thoroughly clean."

"So you had to go for the dustbin to avoid soiling the floor, isn't it?", Jully interrupted and began to laugh again. Amina joined her laughing. They ended up clapping their hands.

"You are right sister, I saw that the dustbin was half filled with dirt. I finally carried it to the gabbage pit."

"Is it the big and very deep one near the male surgical ward?'

"Yes sister. As I was trying to empty its contents into the hole, unfortunately, the bin itself left my hand." The two women burst into another long session of laughter. They laughed and laughed embracing each other and slapping each other's palms.

"It is really very funny, Amina. And what did you do next?"

"You only needed to be there to see my reaction. I screamed as if I was bitten by a poisonous snake." More laughter. "Then I went round looking for help. I had to rescue the dustbin, fast. Sule was still engaged in the N.S' office with the policeman. I would have confessed to him straight away and sought his as-sistance in the first place."

"I can imagine how restless and worried you were, Amina."

"Sure, I looked awful. I couldn't wait for Mallam Sule. I was running to call Philip from the next ward when the P.N.O saw me. He stopped me and sent me to call you for the said meeting. I had no option, but to obey before complaining."

"I now see why you were in such a hurry to go back. You better be on your way right now, before the compound labourers bury it deeper with more gabbage.

"Thank you sister, see you when you come later."

"Goodbye, Amina." They shook hands and took leave of each other.

# CHAPTER TWENTY-THREE

## SULE AND AMINA

AMINA ENTERED THEIR WARD when Sule was just coming out of the toilet room. He was carrying the dirts he gathered there on a small zinc sheet. He was going to throw it into the gabbage pit when he met Amina just at the door.

"Hello! Amina, I didn't know you were at work today."

"Thank you Sule. How could we have met, following the great confusion of this morning?"

"A great confusion indeed. Where are you from?"

"I am just from Jully's house. The P.N.O sent me to call her for an urgent meeting."

"I see."

"But Sule, I saw you briefly this morning. You were going into the N.S' office with a policeman, was anything the matter?"

"Leave them alone, Amina. They were trying to drag me into the case of the missing government revenue."

"You mean the case that originated from the female medical ward during sister Fibina's shift?"

"Exactly that one, you see how trouble wants to follow me?"

"It's a pity Sule, but I hope you have been cleared."

"Why not. False flowers never bear fruits. I was interrogated and searched thoroughly, my sister, but I emerged out clean and white as snow."

"Congratulations. I knew you won't get yourself entangled into such things."

"Thank you my sister. The only thing that worries me now is the where about of my dustbin. Just see what I am now using to pack dirt."

"Oh! Mallam Sule, I am the one to blame", Amina said. Hearing this, Sule's heart leaped in confusion.

"What do you mean, Amina?"

"I mean you need not blame anyone, but me in connection with your lost dustbin."

"Should I take it that you were the one who stole it from the toilet room?"

"I didn't steal it please. Why do you use such a harsh word on me, Sule? Is the dustbin anything worth stealing?"

"If it was nothing worth stealing, why did you remove and hide it then? There is no place in this ward that I have not searched for it."

"I am sorry Sule. You know it was left in the toilet this morning. Immediately I swept and mobbed the floor, that critical patient on bed four was about to vomit. I rushed for the dustbin to avoid soiling the floor too soon. After vomiting into it, I carried that container which was almost half filled with filthy materials out to the garbage pit. I ..."

Amina was still narrating the story when Sule interrupted her.

"What !!", he deeply exclaimed. "Which garbage pit was that? You are lying. Why did you hide the container after emptying it then?"

"Haba Sule, why are you very particular and badly concerned about the dustbin today? Why does the rubbish and dirt in the bin mean much to you. What do I gain by lying to you about them?"

Sule was seriously confused. He didn't know how to answer Amina's questions. He was however obliged to be a bit sober.

"Please Amina, just be sincere to me. Should I trust you that you actually poured the whole content of that container into the pit?"

Amina was bewildered again by such a question from Sule. She wondered what was worth retaining from all the filthy materials of the dustbin which she threw away.

"Let me assure you Sule, that there was nothing worth keeping back from the dustbin as far as I am concerned. You may wish to accept my sincere apology, that even the dustbin itself slipped from my hand and followed its content into the pit."

"Oh sorry!!!", Sule exclaimed. "And so what did you do next? Didn't you make any attempt to recover at least the dustbin?"

"What do you mean by at least the dustbin? What else, apart from the dustbin was worth recovering?"

Sule realized that he had almost betrayed himself. He tried hard to be a bit more tactful in his utterances thereafter.

"Nothing Amina. Infact nothing apart from the dustbin was worth anything. I am worried. Did you recover it?"

"No, Sule. I searched for you, but you were still busy with that armed policeman in the N. S' office. I was running to the next ward to call Philip, when I met with the P.N.O. He straightaway sent me to Jully's house. I was just coming back from the errand when I meet you here."

Sule was a bit relieved. He had hope that his dream treasure might still be lying undiscovered amongst the garbage in the pit.

"Let's hope those cruel compound labourers have not yet buried them deeper down", Sule said.

"Infact you puzzle me, the way you speak today, Sule", Amina said.

"How?"

"What do you mean by 'them' in your last comment? The dustbin and what else?"

"Oh no! I meant to say 'it' and not 'them'." Sule blamed himself for another attempt to betray himself.

"You look confused Sule."

"You are right. The rigorous exercise I underwent in the hand of that cruel policeman is trying to affect my brain."

"I can see that", Amina said.

"By the way, what day is today?" Sule asked in panic and answered it himself. "Today is Friday. Oh God!' it is the day that the compound labourers usually burn off the garbage in the pits."

"Infact that was why I rushed back from the town to seek for quick help. I remembered that the dustbin ran the risk of getting burnt. Something had to be done about it quick."

"You are right, Amina"

"No wonder, I saw smoke high in the sky as I was entering the hospital premises."

"What!!" Sule exclaimed. "Do you know from which of the garbage pit the smoke was coming out?" Sule was terribly worried, not for the dustbin, but for something unknown to Amina.

"Settle down Sule, I know you love that container very much. It appears they have not yet come to the garbage pit into which the bin had fallen. We still have enough time to rescue it, if we act fast."

"Now let us rush there to see what we can do about it. Do you know the where about of the long ladder?"

"Yes, it is behind the T. B ward. Let me run for Philip to help you carry it", Amina said. She was just going to run off when Sule stopped her.

"Just wait a minute, Amina. No need for Philip. I think I can carry it alone with slight help from you."

"Why giving yourself that great burden, Sule?"

"Calling people for help unnecessarily will just mean a weakness on our side."

"You are right, Sule. I don't even want people to know that I was careless", Amina was completely ignorant of the real reason why Sule didn't want publicity during the process of recovering the dustbin. She however had a slight suspicion that there could be something more than the dustbin in Sule's mind. She therefore decided to keep a strict check on Sule during the process of recovering the dustbin.

# CHAPTER TWENTY-FOUR

# THE RESCUE EXERCISE

SULE AND AMINA PROCEEDED to the T. B. ward. They struggled to carry the ladder to the big garbage pit. Unlike Sule, Amina was sweating under the weight of the heavy ladder. She couldn't move fast. Moving faster than her and being in front, Sule seemed to be dragging her along with the ladder fastened to her neck. She endured without complain.

At last they got to the pit. The heavy object was gently lowered into the hole. It was moved here and there until they found a stable position for it.

"I know exactly where the dustbin had dropped." Amina said with a willingness to go down for it. If you don't mind, I could go down to pick it more easily."

"Nonsense, if you were capable of doing so, why did you not do so earlier."

"Mallam Sule, you don't seem to take things kind with me today. What is actually the matter? If it is because I dropped your filth container into the pit, please take it from me that it was not intentional. You don't have to help me remove it, if it pains you to do so. My only problem was how to bring the ladder here. Now that it is here, let me suffer for my mistake. I don't want you to touch the filthy materials below for no fault of yours." Sule was quite ashamed of his hard words on Amina. He tried to be more careful and gentle in his approach.

"Who told you that I don't want to help you or that it pains me to go down and recover the dustbin. The only thing is that you are trying to hurt my manhood."

"How Sule?"

"Haba Amina! How can I bear to see you descend down into the garbage pit to trace the bin from amongst the rotten smelling dirts while I stand here calling myself a man?"

"O.K. I now see what you mean." Amina said smiling.

Sule then descended down into the pit. Amina was curiously watching him from the mouth of the pit. The bottom of the pit was not dark. It was noon time, with the overhead sun throwing its rays straight to the bottom of the pit. The dustbin was slightly covered by some dirt.

Amina saw how Sule pulled out the bin and anxiously glanced into it. It was empty. He hung it unto one of the stick rails of the ladder. Surprisingly, he bent down once more, ransacking the garbage with a piece of stick. She wondered what else he was looking for. She amazingly kept mute.

She soon saw Sule picking up some papers in bundles. The papers appeared almost all of equal size. He quickly pocketed them with a conspicuously shaking limb. His attention was all focused on what he was doing that he didn't look up to see the curious observation being made by Amina from above.

After a few more pushing here and there without seeing more of the essential papers, he picked up the dustbin and climped up the ladder. Just as he emerged from the hole, he unexpectedly met face to face with sergent Fesus, the P.M.O and some hospital security men in addition to Amina.

Amina's attentions was completely buried into the pit, watching Sule's amazing performances below. She didn't notice when those other spectators crept in to watch the cinema together with her. She was also shocked and surprised to see them around. She ignorantly wondered what brought them, but Sule knew exactly why they came.

Sule almost fell back into the pit. He was dumfounded. His

limbs were vibrating as if to produce a tune. The uncalled for visitors had observed all that was happening around the pit. He was caught red handed.

Sergent Fesus was the happiest of all of them. He knew he was right in his guess. The dustbin was the answer to the problem he encountered. After checking Sule and the toilet room, he went home disappointed, but it later occurred to him that there was a dustbin in the toilet earlier.

That container was not there when he had dialogue with Segun in that room. It was there when he found Sule there in the first place. However, when they went to check the toilet room later with the N.S inclusive, the dustbin was not there any longer. That idea only came to him when he went home.

Sule must have tactifully buried the required money amongst the dirt in that container.

Unknown to Sule, Fesus came back tracing the dustbin and that is how they got to the garbage pit. They all tiptoed to the pit silently without distracting Amina's attention.

"Do you still want to deny?", Fesus asked Sule.

"Deny what?" Sule was panic-stricken. His words came out under hard struggles and were faintly audible.

"Deny that you now have the missing government money on you." One of the hospital security men said.

"Well, I can't deny. It could be that I have them. In the process of recovering our dustbin from this pit. I discovered some amounts of money amongst the garbages, I don't know how they got there."

"Bring them out Sule", the P.M.O ordered.

Sule brought out the dirty bundles of Naira notes from his pocket. They were mostly twenty Naira notes. The money was carefully counted and found to be the exact amount.

Amina was taken aback. She now knew why Sule was so

particular and concerned about the contents of the dustbin. Sergent Fesus felt like jumping high to the sky with joy. He was surely going to bag another promotion.

Both Sule and Amina were accused, but Amina was able to defend herself properly before the hospital management and the police. She was acquitted.

Detailed investigations later led to the tracing of all the culprits. All those who were involved were given their fair share of disciplinary actions according to the law. On the other hand, all who performed anything worthy of praise were given their fair share of rewards.

The End